VILLAGE PLANNING
IN THE PRIMITIVE WORLD

PLANNING AND CITIES

PLANNING AND CITIES

General Editor

GEORGE R. COLLINS, Columbia University

VILLAGE PLANNING IN
THE PRIMITIVE WORLD

DOUGLAS FRASER

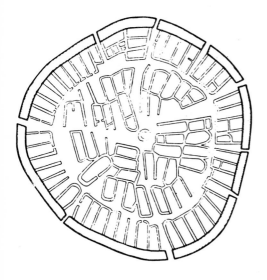

GEORGE BRAZILLER NEW YORK

FOR DAVID, MICHAEL, AND VICTORIA

CONTENTS

ACKNOWLEDGMENTS

Without the generous help and advice of many scholars, colleagues, librarians, and students, this book could never have been written. In particular, I should like to thank Marie Adams, Herbert M. Cole, Sarah Gill, Marianne Forssell Gillberg, Heather von Manowski, Irmgard Moschner, Jeanette Peterson, V. R. van Romondt, Roger Y. D. Tan, Joan Vastokas, and Paul S. Wingert for sharing information and ideas with me. My thanks go also to J. Beguin, Alfred Bühler, Nicholas England, Herta Haselberger, G. J. A. Ojo, Robert F. Thompson, Colin Turnbull, James Walton, and other anthropologists for the use of field data and illustrations, the indispensable currency of this type of scholarship.

I would also like to express my gratitude to Allan Chapman, Esther Dam, Alit Djadjasoebrata, and Adolf Placzek for their assistance in obtaining various books and photographs. I am indebted to the staffs of the American Museum of Natural History; American Geographical Society; Department of Manuscripts, British Museum; Avery Library, Columbia University; Federal Department of Works and Housing, Nigeria; Museum of the American Indian; Museum of Primitive Art; New York Public Library; Provincial Archives, Victoria; Rijksmuseum voor Volkenkunde, Leiden; Tropenmuseum, Amsterdam; and the United Nations Information Service for many kindnesses. Janice Pargh and Cindy Hills of George Braziller, Inc. have my thanks for their hard work and unfailing optimism in the face of obstacles.

I am indebted to the Ford Foundation and the Institute of African Studies, School of International Affairs, Columbia University, for a Faculty Fellowship that enabled me to visit West Africa.

Lastly, I should like to thank George Collins for inviting me to explore this subject and for editing the final manuscript.

Douglas Fraser
Columbia University

GENERAL EDITOR'S PREFACE

The history of cities, of their physical planning, and of man's theories of urbanism represents a facet of cultural history that is particularly meaningful to us in these years of world-wide urban crisis. Clearly, the dimensions and variety of problems that face us as citizens today are infinitely greater than those of any previous civilization. Nevertheless, it is illuminating for us to examine town structures and ideals of other times and places and to determine how they related to the functioning of the society that was being housed.

It is our hope in this series of books to treat many aspects of urban history and to do so efficiently and in depth by inviting a specialist for each volume who can enlighten us from the vantage point of his own field of competence and his personal enthusiasm for it. We have therefore divided the many titles of our intended survey into a number of categories, such as epochs and areas, theories and models, great planners, and so forth. We have urged our authors to dwell especially on the structural, architectural, and formal components of their subject, not only because these factors seem to be disregarded in the precipitate growth of contemporary cities, but also because the literature on these features of urban history is not at the moment easily accessible to students and interested laymen.

We are commencing with books about epochs and areas. In this historical overview we will range from the root beginnings of the process of urbanism, as seen in settlement patterns of "primitive" man and in the rebirth of towns in Europe during the Middle Ages, to the most sophisticated formulae of baroque despots and of contemporary systems analysts.

G.R.C.

INTRODUCTION

No matter where he lives or how, man must juxtapose his dwellings and more specialized structures in some manner. Whether he does this consciously and on a colossal scale, as in modern industrial societies, or with little apparent premeditation, as in the so-called primitive world,[1] is not the issue. For the important thing is the choices that are made and why they come about. These choices are significant because they are symptomatic of the attitudes and values of the community, whether large or small, that accepts the final placement of the buildings. No society, however simple or complex it may be, is privileged in this respect: all reveal themselves equally by their manipulation of habitable space.

At the same time, we must recognize that planning occupies a somewhat different position in the primitive world than it does in the so-called high cultures. In the latter, planning used to function primarily as a mechanism of socio-political or religious control; its chief purpose was to enhance the power of various leaders and institutions by demonstrating their jurisdiction over segments of domestic and ceremonial space. This essentially authoritarian outlook has nowadays been largely supplanted in industrialized societies by an insistence on sanitary, economic, and aesthetic reasons for planning; but the willingness to subordinate the rights of private owners to the commonweal remains as a heritage from an earlier aristocratic era. Primitive societies, on the whole, avoid this problem not by being egalitarian but rather by distributing power among social institutions (lineages, councils of elders, secret societies, etc.) that are hedged about with countless traditional forms of restraint. Marriage, for example, places a man under obligation to his wife's relatives who are already in competition for food or wealth with his own people. So his society may insist that the man work for his wife's relatives and show them lifelong respect. Moreover, these societies tend to oppose an arbitrary exercise of power by a single individual; they encourage cooperation rather than competition among their members. Planning in such groups, therefore, unlike that in the high cultures, is likely to be largely a matter of consensus.

Because of this insistence on general agreement, the planning solutions chosen in primitive societies are usually traditional ones. There is little danger of disagreement, after all, when the solution is a long-established one that has already been approved by the ancestors. This is particularly true in small groups whose concept of history is essentially that of changes of state (from unborn, to living, to ancestor) rather than of dominant personalities. What is more, primitive societies generally believe that the scope of human knowledge is foreordained by a supernatural power and that the original stock of ideas cannot —and should not—be expanded, questioned, or altered.[2] This suggests that innovation in such societies is likely to come about slowly, perhaps as a consequence of unforeseen challenges to the prevailing system.

Yet primitive societies are by no means indifferent to the problem of laying out a village or town. It is characteristic of these societies, though, that formal design-schemes *per se* play little part in their thinking. Whereas industrial societies are constantly adopting plans invented for other regions, the typical primitive society, until recently, had little contact with its neighbors and seldom had any reason to adopt an alien planning system. Each group had access only to the impulses, attitudes, and values circulating within a relatively small circle.

Nevertheless, partly because of this isolation, the range and variety of solutions adopted in the primitive world is staggering. Some groups, such as the Bamileke of the Cameroun Grasslands (Figs. 1–2), use their village layout as a visible paradigm of their social system. Others, such as the Dogon of the western Sudan, mass their dwellings and granaries in bewildering clusters (Fig. 3) that appear to have no connection with the remarkably simple ideal Dogon village plan (Fig. 4) which is modeled on the human figure. Still others, like the Cliff Dwellers and other peoples of the American Southwest, adapted the arrangement of their buildings to suit the site (Figs. 5–10). There seems to be no system or rule that accounts for all cases.

In consequence, it is unwise to approach planning in the primitive world purely as a formal phenomenon. Consider, for instance, the axial plan consisting of two parallel rows of dwellings. This scheme is widespread among maritime peoples in the Pacific islands and is obviously ancient there.[3] But it is also present at A Nato, Vigilo, and Kumbun villages at the southwestern tip of New Britain in Melanesia where "the village houses are now arranged in two or more parallel lines, as a result of government control."[4] Moreover, many inland people such as the Gururumba in the upper Asaro valley of the New Guinea highlands, the Koniagi of Guinea in Africa, and the Karaja of the Amazon basin in Brazil construct their dwellings in two parallel rows.[5] Morphologically these plans all resemble one another, but functionally the differences are enormous. The two Gururumba house-rows are occupied respectively by men and women; the Koniagi rows by unmarried individuals and families; and the Karaja dwellings by individual households of diverse size. Moreover, it is not even certain that these plans are ancient ones, since each of the people in question has recently undergone considerable culture change. The point, in any event, is clear: to discuss village planning in the primitive world merely in terms of formal arrangement is virtually meaningless.

How, then, can one approach the vast, unexplored subject of planning in the primitive world? One alternative to the purely morphological approach is to examine the local attitudes that underlie the preferred plans along with the way the layout expresses and interacts with other aspects of the society. This is the structural-functional method now widely used in anthropological circles. Fundamental to this approach is the assumption that in primitive societies, aspects of culture as seemingly remote from one another as, say, fishing techniques and residence patterns are not necessarily unconnected. Those who employ the structural-functional method try to detect unforeseen relationships between various institutions and to single out underlying attitudes and value patterns behind them.[6] Functional interaction and structural patterns are, of course, peculiar to the area under investigation, and it is difficult, if not impossible, to generalize such observations into rules. But this method provides a better insight into specific village plans than does any purely morphological approach.

In the pages that follow we will examine the village plans of a number of societies from the structural-functional viewpoint. All of these cultures differ radically from one another and from industrialized societies. Each provides, as it were, a case history in which is rehearsed a single solution to the planning problem. For the sake of clarity, only cultures having clear-cut geometric plans are discussed, and these are arranged in a sequence from the simplest to the most complex. This sequence is in no way exhaustive nor can it be used to classify other cultures or planning systems within the primitive world. The selection is an arbitrary one based largely on the availability of descriptive literature. But it is hoped that this sampling of the rich, formal possibilities employed in the primitive world will encourage others to salvage what little remains of a great, varied, but soon-to-be-discarded human heritage.

MBUTI PYGMIES

Prior to the entry of the black African agricultural tribes into the fringes of the Ituri forest a few centuries ago, the Mbuti Pygmies were the only inhabitants of this vast woodland in the north-eastern Congo (see Map A). The Mbuti are still easily distinguished from the rest of the black African population both by their diminutive size, which seldom exceeds four feet, and by their traditional way of life.[7] For the Mbuti are hunters and gatherers who capture game by means of nets or poisoned arrows and collect wild roots, honey, mushrooms, berries, nuts, and fruits in the forest. Pygmies have lived this kind of life for thousands of years, as Egyptian, Greek, and Roman records testify, and only in the last four hundred years or so has their control of this region been challenged by invaders. Even today the Mbuti are the only true forest dwellers of the region, as the agricultural villagers must clear away the natural vegetation in order to plant their crops of manioc, banana, peanuts, corn, rice, beans, and palm oil. In other words, the Pygmies may be said to represent an Old Stone Age (hunting and gathering) way of life, while the villagers, being food producers, have passed through what V. Gordon Childe called the Neolithic Revolution.[8]

The joint occupancy of the Ituri by two peoples having radically different ways of life has had a profound effect on both groups. Mbuti have acquired a taste for plantation foods and for such commodities as iron, pottery, textiles, tobacco, and palm wine, which their own culture does not produce. Conversely, the villager still relies on the Pygmies to get such forest products as game, thatching materials, and medicinal herbs, because his own fear of the forest and lack of woodcraft prevent him from obtaining these things for himself. Pygmies also supply casual labor and occasional entertainment during more prolonged sojourns in the villages. This symbiotic relationship is made possible by the mutual needs of the two groups, but this does not mean that the Pygmies approve of or are subordinated to the sedentary village groups. Indeed, the Pygmies think of the village as a place to be raided and in private refer to the villagers as animals. The Mbuti look upon the village both as a place for relaxation and as potentially dangerous—hot, noisy, and disease-ridden. For them, the forest symbolizes the opposite qualities—tranquillity, social harmony, coolness. The forest is often referred

11

to as Father or Mother and, like the good parent, it provides nourishment, joy, and security for all its children.

Mbuti life-patterns reflect their dual existence. When they go to live with the villagers, the Mbuti sometimes align their camp in imitation of the typical Congo agricultural village (Figs. 11–12), with two or more parallel rows of houses facing each other and a third unit placed where the men's meetinghouse or village chief's residence would ordinarily block off one end.[9] The wattle-and-daub construction technique of the villagers' houses is also imitated by the Pygmy men when building these huts. But this apparent accommodation to the village scheme of things is an illusion. Pygmies have no chiefs, and when they are living in a village, even the Mbuti nuclear family (husband, wife, and children) ceases to function as a unit; nor is there any lineage system operating, such as the villagers might employ in their own orderly layouts. Indeed the Mbuti village-camp plan, like many other Pygmy village-based activities, seems to be a sort of caricature of village life secretly designed to weaken the villagers' hold over the Pygmies. For, as Colin Turnbull, the leading student of the Pygmies, has shown, the Mbuti have developed innumerable ways of circumventing village domination, while at the same time maintaining sufficient ties to make a show of acquiescence profitable.

When the Mbuti return to their natural habitat in the forest, their living patterns undergo a radical transformation. In the Ituri the basic unit is the hunting band comprised of three to thirty nuclear families. This band is a composite group, including members of not one or two but a dozen or more patrilineages who join or leave the band at will. In other words, while distantly related to one another, the members of a Mbuti band have nothing like the lineage cohesion that typifies most co-resident groups in Africa. What, then, holds the Mbuti together?

To live successfully in the forest the overwhelming need is for cooperation: the Mbuti must work together or they will not kill enough game or collect sufficient wild vegetable foods to survive. This principle is articulated, however, not as mere economic necessity but on grounds of the religious and moral order. The Pygmy is taught from infancy to revere the calm of the forest as a model of ethical human behavior. His culture trains him to abhor aggressive or selfish acts that might lead to social disruption. To be sure, Mbuti would not be human if they did not quarrel occasionally with one another, and so their society has evolved a series of relatively passive devices for "signaling" one's irritation without causing an open breach. Several of these involve the plan of the forest camp.

In layout, the Mbuti camp follows no fixed pattern (Fig. 13).[10] Indeed, since the location and membership of the camp change frequently, it appears to be in a constant state of flux. Camps are always sited near a stream, usually in shaded clearings, but the exact shape and dimensions depend on the size of the band at the moment, as well as on the space available. Huts are built entirely by the women, who thrust several bend withes into the ground and cover them with broad leaves for thatch. The placement of the entrance, simply a gap in the withes, is perhaps the most telling decision the woman has to make. If she wishes to express her esteem for some group or individual, she will arrange the entrance so that it faces the other person's hut, the exact orientation depending on the warmth of her regard.[11] But if she is irritated by the behavior of someone in the camp, she will build her door pointing away from that person's house. Should her feelings change once the house is erected, the Mbuti woman may reorient her doorway as many times as she wishes (Fig. 14). In extreme cases she may move to another site, or she and her family may go and live for a while in a village. As a rule, though, members of the camp will attempt quickly to heal the social breach that is obvious to all. In this way the Mbuti camp plan is capable of contributing to social harmony and group cohesion.

Apart from this emphasis on doorways, there are other concepts expressed in the forest layout. Neither the huts nor the entrances to the camp show any orientation with respect to the points of the compass or to the sunrise-sunset axis. Hut entrances, however, do not normally face entirely away from the group (i.e., toward the forest); this awareness of the center finds a parallel in the Mbuti attitude toward the spokesman for a group. When a man talks from his own doorway, he is speaking as an individual and his words carry no more weight than those of his fellows. But if he stands in mid-camp, he is taking the viewpoint of the band.[12] Thus, like so many other people, the Mbuti employ the principle of the center to convey the notion of solidarity and over-all authority. In their case, however, it is significant that the center of the camp is normally void, an expression perhaps of their basic Stone Age egalitarianism.

BUSHMEN

The Bushmen once occupied all of the arid grasslands *(veldt)* of southern and eastern Africa as far north as Tanzania. During the last fifteen hundred years, however, they have been slowly driven back by agricultural and pastoral Bantu-speaking black Africans and by European colonists, until today this remarkable people maintains its traditional way of life only in the inhospitable Kalahari desert and the Okavango swamps of southwestern Africa (see Map A). Racially distinct, the Bushman is also set apart by his language and speech patterns, which employ as many as five different clicking sounds (written as !, #, ", etc.). Like the Pygmies, the Bushmen of southern Africa are food gatherers and hunters; they do not raise any crops or tend herds and do not produce any metalwork or pottery. They represent, in other words, another example of an Old Stone Age culture that has survived into our time.[13]

The members of a Bushman group, at least in the present-day Kalahari, constitute a hunting band; such a unit occupies its own territory and enjoys complete autonomy from all other bands.[14] Each band consists of from eight to sixty people, related by birth or marriage, who utilize the food and water resources of a particular area. People leave the band temporarily to forage for food elsewhere or to visit relatives; but membership in a band is essential to ensure a share of the sparse food and water supply available. The head of each nuclear family (husband, wife, and children) is the father; his authority, while neither formalized nor dictatorial, also extends to the young men who come to live with him to do temporary bride service when they marry his daughters (forming then an extended family).

Authority in the Bushman band rests with a headman who is responsible for controlling food and water resources. Headmanship involves no special regalia, titles, military or juridical power, and the headman receives no particular rewards; the job is inherited by the previous headman's eldest son, unless the latter chooses to renounce it by moving to another band. The principal task of the headman, apart from that of controller of natural resources, is the choosing of the site for a new settlement and the kindling of the ceremonial fire there. If he is too young, too weak, or too old to exercise office, the actual role of leadership may devolve on another man of demonstrated ability. The headman of a Bushman band is therefore only first among equals, and

15

in many ways his function is merely that of inventory-keeper in an area where the miscalculation of resources is tantamount to disaster.

Bushman architecture is consistent in its simplicity with their nomadic way of life. The huts, or *scherms* (windscreens in Afrikaans) consist merely of a score or so of slender branches collected by the women in the bush and thrust into the ground in a crescent pattern (Fig. 15); the tops are then woven together to form a half-hemispherical frame which is covered with loose brush, crude thatch, or grass matting to form a shelter against the heat of the sun and the cool night-breezes of the desert. Such structures are comparable to the windscreens erected by Australian aborigines but are somewhat simpler than the houses of the Mbuti Pygmies described previously.

Among !Kung Bushman groups, settlements (called *werfs* - camps in Afrikaans) do not show many constant features. They are always built within easy reach of supplies of wild vegetable food *(veldtkos)* and a mile or so from the waterhole, so as not to interfere with the local game. The headman has the right to choose the best spot on the site for his own hut. Other people settle down near him, each nuclear family having its own *scherm* with a nearby fire. Huts belonging to members of the same extended family invariably cluster together, but there is no fixed pattern of residence or exact layout of the *werf*. Entrances may point in any direction: toward or away from the prevailing winds, rain, sun, neighbors' *scherms*, or the camp as a whole, depending on the terrain and the whim of the women who build them.[15] The principal exception is the placement of the *≠Kao*, the sleeping hut of the unmarried young men, which is always erected to the east of the headman's dwelling (Fig. 16); the *≠Kao* is placed in the direction of the boys' initiation camp, which is usually a quarter of a mile or so to the east of the *werf*.[16] The easterly axis is apparently a sacred one for the Bushman, since the supreme god lives in the east and the god of the initiation rites comes from that direction to attend the ceremony. This awareness of orientation with respect to the rising sun is perhaps the most notable feature of !Kung Bushman planning. Records of other Bushman groups, while less complete, indicate that the concept of solar orientation was also widely recognized by the Bushmen of old. Sixty years ago Stow reported that the groups then living in South Africa built their *scherms* in an irregular ring with the entrances all oriented toward the east; the home of the headman was unusually large and was surrounded by elaborate rock paintings. Similarly, Ellenberger states that "when possible, the entrance faced the east, so as to catch the first rays of the morning sun."[17]

Among the modern Heikum Bushmen, neighbors of the !Kung to the west, the headman selects his homesite near a central tree where the first fire will be lighted and where the men will subsequently hold their meetings. Only the headman and his brother (potential successor among the Heikum) may live near this tree. The remaining members of the band set up *scherms* in a semicircle on the opposite side of the tree from the headman's hut, leaving space for the dancing ground in the middle. Adolescent boys and girls live in huts built on opposite sides near the center of the *werf;* married daughters of the headman erect their *scherms* as far away from the headman as possible because of the parent-in-law taboos observed in this society. Thus several social groupings involving opposition (headman—populace, boy—girl, parent-in-law—child) find expression in axial separation. This indicates that the Bushmen, unlike the Pygmies, not only knew the concept of the center, but also used solar orientation and axial alignments in their *werfs* to express social and religious attitudes and values.

CHEYENNE INDIANS

In common with other nomadic buffalo-hunting tribes of North America, the Cheyenne were relatively recent arrivals in the Great Plains area. Until the end of the seventeenth century, they lived in the woodlands of Minnesota, not far from the Great Lakes. But at that time they migrated westward and soon adopted a sedentary, agricultural way of life, growing maize, beans, and squash in the valleys of the upper Missouri River (see Map C). Hunting by means of buffalo drives provided only a seasonal supplement to their diet. This pattern persisted up to the mid-eighteenth century, at which time Plains culture began to be radically altered by the introduction of the horse. Mounted on horseback, the Cheyenne and other Plains Indians could pursue the buffalo across the nearly waterless high Plains and carry back enough meat to camp to survive the severest winter.

Thus by 1830 the Cheyenne had completely abandoned agriculture and the security of village life in favor of nomadic buffalo-hunting. This new mode of existence, accompanied by the introduction of guns and the pressure of European settlement, forced the Cheyenne to become increasingly warlike, the climax being General Custer's defeat in the Battle of the Little Big Horn in 1876. Yet for all their incredible determination and bravery in the face of superior weapons and decreasing buffalo herds, the Cheyenne ultimately had no alternative but to submit first to captivity and deportation, then finally to the humiliations of reservation life.[18] Thus, while the Cheyenne have not always been nomadic hunters, their way of life departed strikingly from that of sedentary food producers.

In its heyday, Cheyenne social organization revolved around a tribal council consisting of forty-four peace chiefs who served for ten years. Each chief was the headman of an extended family and represented one of the ten main Cheyenne bands. The latter units (Fig. 17) lived and hunted alone except when assembled at the time of the Sun Dance and other major communal undertakings. Each band consisted of one or more kindreds (bilateral descent groups) which in turn were comprised of families (headman, his wives, unmarried children, married daughters, their husbands and unmarried children, as well as other relatives). The members of kindreds lived in close proximity to one another and cooperated in economic and ritual activities.

Several Cheyenne institutions cut across the kindreds and

bands, including warriors' clubs and women's societies. These were ungraded social and ritual organizations which fostered awareness of certain common experiences, usually symbolized by means of relics. Such societies functioned also in part as ethical institutions upholding the virtues of bravery in men and chastity in women which the Cheyenne so greatly admired. At certain times in the year special lodges *(tipis)* were set up by the members of these societies in order to perform their songs, dances, and other rituals. Each of the warrior-clubs had four leaders who were the main war chiefs of the tribe. If a war chief was promoted to the ranks of the forty-four tribal peace chiefs, he had to resign his office (although not his membership) in the warrior group.

The Cheyenne also had several ceremonies that symbolized their cohesion as a tribe, the foremost being that of Renewal of the Sacred Arrows. This rite took place approximately at the summer solstice when the life-giving forces of the sun reached their peak. The entire Cheyenne people, dressed in their finest regalia, assembled on one campground, approaching it from the east and singing their songs of joy. After erecting their *tipis* in a prescribed order, the camp fell silent while the priests unwrapped the sacred Medicine Arrows which symbolized the tribal soul. The rites were designed to cleanse and revitalize the community, and only men of the utmost moral virtue could perform them. Upon completion of the Renewal ceremony, a great communal buffalo hunt took place.

Another Cheyenne ceremony of comparable significance was the Sun Dance, which was known throughout the Plains. The purpose of this rite was world renewal.[19] During the ceremonies the priest symbolically recreated the five worlds of the Cheyenne cosmology, beginning with a barren earth which has to be stocked successively with water, vegetation, buffalo, and healthy, happy Cheyenne. Another ritual, the Animal Dance, followed a similar pattern, although during it there was much clowning and good fun. These ceremonies were not necessarily given annually but depended on the presence of an individual who pledged himself (particularly when he or a relative faced death) to undertake the responsibilities of sponsoring a particular rite.

At the times when they assembled as one tribe for ritual purposes, the Cheyenne grouped their dwellings according to a fixed plan. This layout, one used by most Plains Indians, consisted of a large "C"-shaped ring opening toward the east.[20] As many as a thousand *tipis*, three and four deep, formed a circle a

mile or so in diameter (Fig. 18). For the Medicine Arrow Renewal ceremony, the opening in the ring was oriented toward the
rising sun (northeast) as was the entrance of each *tipi*, in order
that the sun's first rays might shine into the lodge. The camp
circle was compared to the circle of stars in the heavens and to a
gigantic *tipi*, the door of which faced east.[21] In recent times,
however, Cheyenne *tipis* have been set up with the entrances
facing the central Sun Dance lodge.[22]

Tradition also governed the location of tribes, bands, and
kindreds on the campgrounds. When the Cheyenne joined the
Ogalala, Sans Arc, Miniconjous, and Hunkpapa for the Battle
of the Little Big Horn, each tribe pitched its own east-facing
camp circle in a row, with the Cheyenne occupying the downstream (northernmost) position (Fig. 19). Similarly, after the
Suhtai (or Sutayo) combined forces with the Cheyenne in 1831,
the former always occupied a particular place on the camp circle
(Fig. 20). Unfortunately, the location of sub-groups in the Cheyenne camp circle is a matter of disagreement (Fig. 21);[23] but
the principle of assigning each band a fixed spot is well doc-
umented for the Cheyenne and for all other Plains groups save
the Blackfoot. There were several privileged locations, notably
the south side near the eastern opening, which seem to have
been sacred; all special lodges, moreover, occupied prominent
spots within the circle. Only the great council *tipis* for the meeting of the forty-four peace chiefs (and, more recently, the Sun
Dance lodge) were erected in the center (Fig. 22).

The emphasis on plan seen in Cheyenne camp circles reflects
customs widely observed throughout the Plains. Among the
Omaha, Ponka, Osage, Kansas, Iowa, Oto, and Missouri, for
example, two sub-groups always occupied the opposite halves
of the camp circle. According to Kansas belief, the road through
a permanent village formed an imaginary east-west axis. Out-
ward bound, the two main halves of the Omaha tribe camped
with their leaders at the two sides of the opening; on the return
journey the leaders became the rear guard, the opening being
reversed to face the line of march (Fig. 19). Among the Omaha,
sacred *tipis* were always pitched in the same relative position,
that is, on the south side, whether moving east or west.[24] On ordinary occasions, Osage camps and *tipis* faced the sunrise; but
if a hunt or raid in which life was to be taken was in progress,
the opening of the circle faced west—the imaginary course was
then toward the sunset, the land of the dead. Among the Kiowa,
the Ree Indians occupied the place of honor immediately south

of the entrance, while the Kiowa proper, who were in charge of the main Sun Dance *tipi*, camped on the western side of the circle.[25] According to Teit, the Coeur d'Alêne occupied a position in the circle corresponding to the geographical location of their homelands.[26]

All of this makes it clear that the Plains Indians, including the Cheyenne, were acutely aware of center, axis, and direction. Whether this awareness stemmed from an older, river-basin heritage or developed after the people had adopted a nomadic way of life is impossible now to determine. But the Cheyenne circle shows the capacity of people living at a food-gathering level to organize their dwelling sites on a colossal scale by means of a combination of axial and centralized alignment.

HAIDA OF THE PACIFIC NORTHWEST

Food gathering, compared with food producing, generally permits only a marginal existence. Large food surpluses are difficult for food gatherers to acquire and store for any length of time. But there are a few food-gathering societies, particularly favored by nature, that long ago achieved a state of economic security comparable to that of sedentary cultivating groups. Perhaps the outstanding example was the people of the Pacific Northwest who lived on the islands and fiords between Puget Sound and Yakutat Bay in southern Alaska (see Map C). Best known for their famous "totem poles," the Indians of this area depended upon fishing, sea-mammal hunting, and shellfish gathering for their livelihood; yet they enjoyed material abundance and a rich ceremonial life. What made this way of life possible was the vast runs of salmon, olachen, and other fish that annually surged up the local rivers to spawn. By harvesting this "crop" with nets, traps, and weirs, Northwest Coast tribes such as the Kwakiutl, Bella Coola, Tsimshian, Tlingit, and Haida acquired enormous food surpluses which they were able to preserve by means of smoking and drying for use later in the winter months.

During the latter period, initiation societies and prominent leaders staged melodramatic dances at which quantities of food and other forms of wealth were consumed or distributed. Many of these dances took the form of ceremonial quests, in which an individual deliberately set out to encounter a particular animal-spirit that ostensibly had conferred "power" on one of his ancestors. Power—essentially the right to perform certain dances, to sing various songs, and to depict the image of the animal-spirit on one's possessions—was in fact usually inherited; the pro forma quest merely served to validate an individual's claims to his legacy.

As an example of the Northwest Coast village, we may single out the Haida town of Ninstints which formerly flourished on Anthony Island, at the southern tip of the Queen Charlotte Islands of British Columbia (Fig. 23). Like most Northwest Coast winter villages (Fig. 24), Ninstints consisted of a single row of large, durable, rectangular houses built of cedar planks; the line of the house fronts paralleled that of the foreshore.[27] This type of plan, characteristic of virtually every Northwest Coast group except the Quinalt of the state of Washington, clearly indicates the maritime orientation of the people.[28] During the winter, several Haida lineages converged on Ninstints for weeks of feasting and dancing. Each of these lineages had its own chief, its own fishing grounds, and berry patches where the members spent their summer months building up the food surplus. All Haida lineages traced descent through the mother and all belonged either to the Eagle or to the Raven moiety (or half). These moieties were exogamous, meaning that a man from one of the Raven lineages was forbidden to marry any woman whose lineage did not belong to the Eagle half; a marriage between Ravens or between Eagles was considered incestuous. Houses, whether winter or summer, were owned by lineages, but only in wintertime, as a rule, were two or more lineages brought into direct confrontation, as at Ninstints. This juxtaposition was necessary, as it enabled the two moieties to exchange brides and undertake other ceremonies, such as the installation of chiefs; members of other lineages were needed on these occasions to serve as an audience for the rites and to receive gifts that sanctioned and recorded the event. When another lineage faced a similar task, the roles were merely reversed.

The complementary relationship of the two Haida moieties is evident at Ninstints in the relative equality of the placement of house sites; having no over-all chief, neither Eagles' nor Ravens' houses dominated the settlement in a planning sense.[29] This is not to say that all lineages were of equal importance or rank: at Ninstints there were at least two Raven lineages (the Striped-Town People and the Sand-Town People), both of which were further divided into sub-lineages. The Striped-Town People owned five houses there and the Sand-Town People four; the two Eagle lineages (Those Born up the Inlet and Those Born at Kunghit) owned four and six houses respectively. The only group not divided into sub-lineages—Those Born up the Inlet—owned the village site which Europeans called Ninstints after one of the Inlet lineage chiefs.

Ninstints village was sited on a straight terrace or midden directly facing the only still water in the area, the tidal basin with its sheltering offshore islet (Fig. 25). Houses 3 through 12 were aligned in a gentle curve and probably constituted the main street of the old village. Houses 13 through 17 represented an expansion into the less-favored, somewhat swampy site where the village obtained its drinking water. This second row of houses, however, included one of the two dwellings (dotted lines) believed to represent an older type of house. One of the most important structures, Chief Ninstints' mortuary house, is believed to be at No. 9 in the first row.[30] Houses 1 and 2 were perhaps later and somewhat arbitrary additions to the plan. Two of the nineteen houses reported to have been owned by the Ninstints lineages are missing; but these may have been lost in the swamp, where a single mortuary pole still stands sixty feet north of No. 17.

Haida villages had no fixed boundaries or encircling stockades. Nevertheless, they were extremely compact. Ninstints dwellings, averaging about thirty-five feet square, were set only two to seven feet apart; thus the littoral was as densely inhabited as a modern trailer camp.[31] If a census of 1835–41, for example, is reliable, 308 people (87 men, 79 women, 68 boys, and 74 girls) lived there then in twenty houses, giving an average of 15.4 per dwelling, or approximately one person per seventy-five square feet of interior space. The extraordinary wind velocities and considerable rainfall in the Queen Charlotte Islands may have encouraged the people to live in such close proximity. But this was not necessarily done for practical reasons alone. Early photographs of Haida villages disclose a tendency to mass these dwellings in a relatively orderly manner with equal stress on the individual structure and on the ensemble. No Haida house completely dominated its neighbors, as was true among the Kwakiutl, nor were buildings as freely dispersed as in Tlingit, Nootka, and Salish villages. Thus despite a lack of centralized authority, Haida planning seems to have been almost baroque in its capacity to reconcile diverse elements into an organic and overriding unity.[32]

The Ninstints village plan, besides emphasizing social and aesthetic cohesion, also reveals underlying aspects of Haida belief. None of the buildings at Ninstints was set aside solely for ritual; nor is this surprising among a people who did not worship deities or ancestors. The Haida employed mythology mainly to glorify lineages, or prominent lineage leaders, and thus had no need for shrines, men's houses, or temples. Rank was calculated within the lineage, and the rights of that lineage were clearly expressed by means of crest symbols—the so-called totem animals—that were carved and painted on its houses and other possessions. The status of lineages was also fixed by custom, leaving little doubt as to its prerogatives. Thus there was an orderliness to the Haida way of life, a preference for clarity and structure at the expense of spontaneity and random association.

For a food-gathering society, Haida village planning seems to

25

be extraordinarily sophisticated. Neighboring peoples whose ecology, social organization, and way of life were essentially similar, never attained the artistic heights reached by the Haida. In recent years scholars have shown the likelihood of early high-culture influences on the Haida, probably stemming from ancient China.[33] There is no reason, however, to suppose that the characteristic plan of the Haida owes anything to that source, as such plans are common among maritime people the world over.

MAILU, NEW GUINEA

New Guinea is one of the least densely populated areas of the world (see Map B). Its high mountains and pestilential swamps, combined with rapid soil depletion due to the torrential rains, have prevented the people of this region from achieving the degree of socio-political centralization found in the adjacent tropical territories of Indonesia and Polynesia. Until European contact, New Guinea villages were more or less cut off from all but a few other hamlets, with which they maintained trade relations. Within each village, there was usually a sharp cleavage between masculine and feminine activities, the men devoting themselves largely to trade, head-hunting, and rituals, while the women carried the burden of gardening, cooking, child care, and housekeeping. Dozens of languages are spoken in the island, the principle distinction being between the Austronesian (Malayo-Polynesian) and non-Austronesian tongues.

The Mailu-speaking people occupy the coastal regions of southeastern New Guinea from Cape Rodney to about the middle of Orangerie Bay. Like the majority of New Guinea peoples, they gain their living by growing root- and tree-crops such as yams and bananas. Some Mailu live in fortified hilltop villages situated several miles inland, but the majority dwell either at the edge of river estuaries or on nearby offshore islands, such as the island of Mailu.[34] Scarcely a mile in diameter, this tiny volcanic islet nevertheless harbors about five hundred and fifty people who live in a single, carefully laid-out village (Figs. 26–28). The Mailu Islanders do not rely for their living on horticulture alone. The men fish extensively, while the women produce an abundance of excellent pottery which the men transport in large sailing canoes up and down the coast. The Mailu act as middlemen, exchanging their handsomely decorated wares for shell and feather ornaments, netted bags, fish, dogs, and pigs, which they then redistribute among coastal and hinterland peoples. Voyages of three hundred miles or more, lasting three months, are commonplace. This pattern of seasonal voyaging for purposes of trade is one which the Mailu share with other coastal tribes in the dry belt of south New Guinea, notably the Motu of Port Moresby who make similar journeys to exchange pots for sago with the Elema of the Papuan Gulf.[35] In both instances the traders' maritime cultural orientation enables them to garner a good living where a purely horticultural way of life would barely support the population.

The Mailu layout is an outstanding example of a type of village plan that is widespread in the Pacific (Fig. 28). The houses of the Mailu are normally arranged in two orderly rows parallel to and about thirty yards from the high-water mark on the beach.[36] Between the two rows is a long cleared space, some thirty to fifty feet wide, which constitutes the village street (Fig. 29). The fronts of the houses always face this street, which is swept daily by the women and, like the rest of the environs of the village, is kept entirely free of vegetation. This street is used mainly as a thoroughfare and for dancing and the ceremonial preparation of food. Houses are of uniform height and decoration, except for men's clubhouses (dubu), which in the past were aligned transversely and stood in the middle of the village street. Each patrilineal clan had at least one of these clubhouses, and each clan occupied its own segment of the village. On Mailu Island the four clans from west to east are Morau, Maradubu, Urumoga, and Bodeabo. The village community jointly owns the land and fishing rights, but hunting rights and other privileges are clan owned; clans are also important as the principal ceremonial units in marriage or funeral rites. Sub-clans, consisting of several families, are also of economic significance since fishing nets and large sailing canoes, which require considerable labor to repair and operate, are jointly owned by the sub-clans. Each clan and sub-clan is led by a headman whose principal task is organizing and executing collective undertakings such as warfare and feasts.

The hierarchy of social organization and economic activity clearly parallels the Mailu village plan. The over-all axial layout corresponds to the level of village organization expressed in corporate ownership of the land, control of the water supply (obtained from a single sink-hole on the island), and collective warfare. The street segments, punctuated by clubhouses and usually slightly set off from one another, are comparable to the role of the clan with its jurisdiction over marriage, residence, and inheritance patterns. Sub-clans, with their own headmen, inheritance rights, jointly-owned canoes and fishing gear, cluster their houses within the portion of the village occupied by their clan. Finally, the members of an extended family form a unit and live in one or more houses set very close together. In other words, for each level of social integration there exists a corresponding spatial expression of unity.

The Mailu plan also suggests the importance of kinship in allocating property and other forms of wealth in a food-producing society. Every inch of the Mailu island and every major human and natural resource on it belong to one social group or another, depending on circumstances. Unique and indispensable resources, such as water supply, belong to the community at large. Title to permanent possessions—lands and the like—is vested in on-going social units such as the clan, while control of more perishable yet immediately productive commodities, including fishing nets and canoes, rest with the lower sub-clans. The greatest power of all—the capacity of young women to reproduce mankind— while seemingly a function of the individual household, is actually linked through kinship and the rules of clan (and sub-clan) exogamy to much higher levels of social organization.

In layout, the Mailu plan resembles that of many other Oceanic peoples. The Roro, for example, northwest of Port Moresby, employ a similar design consisting of two parallel rows of houses confronting one another, with distinctive men's houses at either end of the rows (Fig. 30).[37] But the Roro system is based on two moieties (halves) which occupy opposite sides of the street, and their plan therefore is not so close to Mailu's as it first appears to be. Nevertheless, the parallel layout occurs in so many coastal areas of New Guinea (Figs. 31–33), Melanesia, Micronesia, and Polynesia that this scheme must be linked in some fundamental way to maritime life in the Pacific. The clearest link between such cultures is their skill as voyagers and their dedication to fishing and trading, in contrast to more shore-bound activities like gardening. The majority of New Guinea peoples engaged in this maritime way of life speak Austronesian (Malayo-Polynesian) languages; thus scholars tend to link maritime cultural orientation to the Austronesians, regarded as relative latecomers, who dispersed throughout the Pacific from about 2000 B.C. to A.D. 1000.[38] The people of Mailu do not speak Austronesian, but their decidedly maritime orientation suggests they too should be classified as comparatively recent arrivals in their present area. This may indicate that the parallel alignments of the sort seen at Mailu and Roro are to be ascribed to Austronesian influence.

TROBRIAND ISLANDERS, NEW GUINEA

In the pre-colonial era, the majority of New Guinea societies had no hereditary, paramount leaders or over-all village chiefs; authority in most cases was vested in lineage headmen, skilled organizers, or councils of elders. An exception to this rule, however, existed in the Massim District, the area comprising the eastern tip of New Guinea together with a number of offshore islands (see Map B). In one of these groups, the Trobriand Islands, for example, chiefs held their office by right of birth, and their authority over people of lesser rank was all but absolute. Commoners were forbidden to stand at a level higher than that of the chief[39] or even to decorate their storehouses.

That the Trobriand chief's superiority was indicated also in the layout of his village may be seen from the plan of Omarakana, home of the principal chief of the Kiriwina district (Fig. 34). Located nearly two miles inland from the coast, Omarakana village was sited on a flat, fertile plain covered with scrub and patches of denser vegetation, and consisted of two concentric circles of buildings.[40] The outer circle was composed of houses (bulaviyaka) occupied by the married people; all daily activities such as cooking, gossiping, and eating took place here. Certain closed covered storehouses (sokwaypa), used for inferior yams, and the houses of widows and widowers (bsala nakada'u) were also placed in this ring. Each of these buildings fronted toward the center of the village, although their orientation was not very precise. The inner circle consisted of ceremonial yam storehouses (bwayma); these differed notably in construction from ordinary dwellings because they were more solidly built and had saddle-shaped roofs (Fig. 35). Besides the ceremonial yam houses, the inner ring also contained some bachelors' houses (bukumatula) and houses of the chief's kinsmen (lisiga). In the center of Omarakana village were the burial ground, the dance ground, the chief's hut, and his own yam house—the most impressive structure of all, decorated with carved designs painted red, black, and white, and animal figures set on sticks. Together with the circle of yam houses, the center was sacred and was the focus of masculine ceremonial activities, in contrast to the mundane concerns of the outer ring. No cooking, for example, was carried on in the central area.

The physical organization of Omarakana was largely controlled by the chief's social relations. Houses lying between points A and

B (that is, the southwest) were occupied by the wives of the chief; dwellings between points A and C (east) by his maternal kinsmen, the members of his sub-clan, all of whom claimed ownership of the village. In the third or northern section, B-C, lived commoners who were neither his kinsmen nor his children; these people either justified their citizenship on mythological grounds or, if they were the chief's hereditary servants, lived in the village by right and title but had no claim to its ownership. Their houses were arranged in an orderly fashion comparable to the arrangement of the dwellings of the chief's wives. Only the dwellings of the maternal kinsmen, with attendant bachelor houses, tended to depart from circularity in the settlement pattern. This deviation is interesting both in aesthetic and social terms, for in Trobriand art the prevailing designs are curvilinear, though seldom, if ever, precisely circular.[41] By the same token, it is the maternal kin groups who, as Malinowski points out, are most often at odds with the chief, owing to the conflict between the rules of matrilineal descent and inheritance and the chief's natural tendency to shower benefits and privileges on his own children. This conflict seems to be illustrated in the more irregular placement of kinsmen's houses and yam houses in Omarakana.

The orderly circular plan of Omarakana and the stress on decorated storehouses in the Trobriands is unusual in Melanesia, where men's meetinghouses were generally the most important buildings. In part, this is attributable to structural-functional factors: Trobriand chiefs collected enormous annual revenues from their constituents, and the open-walled yam house served as much to display his wealth as to store it. Under the hieratic Trobriand system, village chiefs and sub-clan headmen contributed regularly to the support of the district chief, who had as many as sixty wives and five dozen tributary communities. The more wealth a chief possessed, the greater his power and prestige and the more marriages he could undertake.[42] Besides controlling weather and fishing magic, a Trobriand chief was entitled to have commoners do the heavy work of gardening, house-building, and fishing for him and to have them carry him when he was tired. Thus Malinowski interprets the superior design of the chief's yam houses on a purely structural-functional basis as "an index and symbol of power."

But to attribute the distinctive appearance of Trobriand yam houses and, by implication, their layout solely to local factors, as Malinowski does, is to overlook a wealth of evidence suggesting the intrusive character of many Trobriand concepts. Saddle-roofed storehouses with decorated gables are particularly characteristic of the Karo Batak (Figs. 36–37), Toba Batak, and Minangkabau of Sumatra, the Toradja of Celebes (Figs. 38–39), and other conservative peoples of Indonesia. Decorated storehouses of almost identical appearance are depicted on two-thousand-year-old metal drums used by the Bronze-Iron Age Dongson culture of greater Southeast Asia.[43] Named for its typesite in Tonkin, the Dongson culture apparently dominated mainland and insular Southeast Asia during the second half of the first millennium B.C. Its characteristic metal artifacts—kettle drums, socketed axes, and ceremonial weapons—have been found over a vast area ranging from south China to western New Guinea. From the continued prominence of saddle-roofed houses, ships of the dead, spiral ornaments, and other traits in conservative Indonesia, many scholars have concluded that Dongson played the role of "mother culture" to all Southeast Asia long before Indian and Chinese influences permeated the area.[44] A number of traits still widespread in Indonesia—strong chieftainship, fastidious curvilinear ornament, and orderly layouts—are apparently the products of this Dongson heritage. Since many Trobriand art forms (hocker figures, wooden sword clubs, spiral designs, canoe-prow ornaments) find their closest parallels in the art of the Indonesian Dongson cultures,[45] it seems reasonable to view the exceptional saddle-roofed store houses and centralized village plan of the Trobriands as expressing similar links with the Dongson tradition of Southeast Asia.

SOUTH NIAS ISLANDERS, INDONESIA

Some seventy-five miles off the northeast coast of Sumatra lies the large mountain-covered island of Nias (see Map B). This island nurtured a culture of barbaric splendor that, although mentioned over a thousand years ago in Persian and Arabic texts, has only become well known during the present century. One reason for this isolation was the rugged physical environment of Nias, with its fringing reefs, jungle-covered hills, and dense stands of man-high grasses. Equally if not more important, however, was the concerted hostility of the Nias people to outside incursions; tribes that ordinarily engaged in mutual head-hunting banded together to meet the threat of foreign domination. Unlike some of their neighbors, the people of Nias have continued to flourish even after the Dutch established nominal control in 1904; a recent census placed their number at over 200,000. They gained their livelihood by growing taro, maize, yams, and rice, by raising pigs, chickens, and carabao for sacrifices, and, until recently, by selling slaves to importers from Sumatra. In addition, the men, even chiefs, engaged in gold- and copper-smithing and woodcarving, while pottery making and weaving were the exclusive province of women.[46]

Nias social organization and religion were closely intertwined. In south Nias, where several lineages occupied a single village, there was a main chief and a series of lesser chiefs, each representing a lineage and the hamlet it occupied. Chiefs were regarded as having quasi-divine status during their lifetime, and after their death, they were believed to occupy a special heaven where they lived in a state commensurate with the splendor of the funeral sacrifices performed in their behalf.

The gulf between chief and commoners in Nias was considerable, although village elders, chosen from among the latter, sat as a council in matters having to do with the *adat* (customary law). These gatherings took place in the village square or at the chief's house, both sacred spots where, in typically Indonesian fashion, the old men met to determine what the *adat* required. Failure to adhere to the *adat* led to immediate divine and ancestral retribution in the form of disease and misfortune. Slaves, while low in the religious system—they could be killed if the owner so decided—rarely suffered any hardship, being considered a valuable form of wealth. They were not entitled to take heads in raids or to wear the neck ornaments distinctive of the successful head-hunter. Head-hunting was particularly important in the second-burial rites, since the heads were rubbed against the coffin (*owo*=boat) to revive the soul of the deceased.

Nias religion was fundamental to almost every aspect of island life, including village planning. Reduced to its essentials, this religion was a dualistic one, constructed around certain polar-opposite pairs such as sky/earth, sun/moon, masculine/feminine, world tree/world snake, upriver/downriver, metallic hardness/textile pliability.[47] These opposites were symbolized by two brother deities, Lowalani (Lowalangi) and Latura Dano (Lature Dano), the one identified with the upper world, the other with the underworld. Lowalani was linked with the sun, life, light, the cock, yellow (gold) and goodness; while to his opponent were assigned the moon, death, darkness, the serpent, black, and evil. Despite their diametrical relationship, these two deities were necessary complements to one another and by no means mutually exclusive. Indeed, study of Nias ritual suggests that the most sacred occasions required the achievement of equilibrium between these opposing forces.

In Nias cosmology, the world consisted of nine layers, on the uppermost of which Lowalani resided with his wife, Silewe Nazarata, who was also described as sister to the two brothers. She created the earth and was mediator between the two deities and human beings. She was identified with priests and priestesses, and she imparted wisdom and understanding to mankind. But at the same time, Silewe Nazarata was a notorious trickster-prankster associated with the underworld. She apparently epitomized the ambivalent dualistic-monistic structure of the Nias cosmos. Important, too, was the world tree *(eho)* which symbolized the cosmos and the village. The boundaries of the village, synonymous with those of the cosmos, were supposedly marked with wood from the *eho*. Noblemen were said to reside in its branches, and the good man (that is, the man who gives feasts) was compared with the bounteous world tree. Beneath the tree, yet sometimes identical with it, was the world snake (i.e., Milky Way, rainbow, primeval river, crocodile) on whose back the dead traveled to the underworld.

The overwhelming emphasis on cosmic symbols in Nias is the key to human and spatial relations in the area. The south Nias name for a chief, *si ulu* ("that which is up river") indicated his cosmic superiority, while the lowest class of slaves (those who resided permanently in the fields) were held in contempt because they lived outside the cosmos (village) and were therefore scarcely human in terms of the Nias world order. Slaves that lived in the village were forced to live under the house (also a cosmos in miniature) along with pigs and other animals. Commoners occupied the spatial equivalent of the underworld, counterbalancing the position of chiefs in the upper world.

The Nias village was synonymous in the minds of the people with the cosmos; indeed, the word for village *(bahmua)* means "sky" or "world". South Nias villages were almost invariably sited on hilltops, partly for defensive reasons and partly for symbolic purposes; they were reached by ascending many stone steps and terraces leading to a broad central village street (Figs. 40–41). This street formed the main axis of the town and was oriented from east to west or north to south, or occasionally in other directions. The axis was independent of the location and course of the river usually found nearby.[48] Several thousand people sometimes inhabited a single south Nias village, but the plan was essentially the same for all settlements, large or small. Opposite the entrance was a vast open rectangle with perhaps forty pile-built houses lining either side and a chief's house at the end. Since this oblong was usually broken by many terraces, the chief's house rose monumentally above all other buildings. Chiefs' houses were larger and finer in construction than other dwellings, one chief's house having taken five years to build. Numerous altars, stone seats *(osa osa)* dedicated to the ancestors, columns *(behoe)* vaguely comparable to Greek hermes, and stones *(niogadji)* shaped like the capitals of columns, were placed on terraces in front of important houses throughout the square. These monuments commemorated the specific ancestors whose souls resided in them, but the chief who paid for the attendant rites gained measurably in prestige. The terraces were often paved and framed with retaining walls, thus creating open spaces in front of each house comparable to the vast, open oblong facing the chief's house at the end.

The over-all dimensions of the Nias village square and the proportion of its length to its width seem to have been flexible.[49] What remains fixed is the prevailing axial and cosmic aspect of the plan. The chief's house is invariably located at the upper end of the street; this feature stems from the Nias conception of space as upriver/downriver and sunrise/sunset. For Nias cosmology, like that of many regions, is less concerned with actual directions than with symbolic ones. Space is measured with respect to the chiefs. Thus the end they occupy is called Sibaloi (or "upper reaches of river") and this is opposite, and opposed to, *Jou* (downstream, the entrance to the village). On the nobleman's right, facing downstream, is the region of sunrise *(abolata)* and on his left *(aechula)* that of the sunset. The latter area is identified with the dead, whereas the right-hand region, that of sunrise, is linked with life, light, and the emergent sun. The directions, however, are conventional ones; thus, although the nobility ordinarily is synonymous with south *(raja)* so that the east is on their right hand, the actual location of their section may be to the north of the commoners. In other words, space in Nias is plotted relative to the aristocracy of the village rather than, as in our own world, by reference to fixed geodetic coordinates.

The ceremonies that accompanied the founding of a Nias village also indicate its cosmic character. After having selected a suitable site, performed certain rites, and seen that the land was clear of trees and dense vegetation, the priest in charge laid out the limits of the village square, using reputed pieces of the world tree as markers, as we have seen. Anyone who subsequently removed one of these markers was punished by a fine. At the center of the oblong was located the Fuso Newali (navel of the village), that is to say, the center from which the limits of the village were measured. According to Møller, only the village square, with its surrounding houses, was actually planned in this way (Fig. 42).[50]

The Nias village plan is not merely modeled on the cosmos; it has all the symbolic attributes of the world. For example, the stone stairways leading to the village are carved with images of crocodiles, lizards, and other symbols of the lower world, some of them devouring fish, dogs, and other animals. This end of the village *(Jou)* is regarded as "downstream," which is synonymous with death, commoners, aquatic animals, "west" and "north." Sibaloi, or "river source, upstream," corresponds to life, chieftainship, aerial creatures, "east," "south," and the sun. The village axis is further conceived of as the sky-river, or world axis, which runs between upper world and underworld. This sky-river is both the cosmos and the world snake (i.e., the Milky Way) that rings the world (or village). The world tree grows at the center of the "universe," the Fuso Newali, at which spot the fusion of opposing forces is believed to take place. Such joinings or reconciliations characterize the climactic moments in Nias thought.

One problem remains to be discussed. Suzuki maintains that the emphasis on the world tree and world snake indelibly mark Indian influence on Nias culture. This may be true, but the fundamental ideas of the upper and lower worlds, the bird/serpent,

masculine/feminine, upriver/downriver, sunrise/sunset opposi-
tions do not appear to be specifically Indian, although many
parallels exist in Indian thought. For these concepts occur again
and again among non-Indianized peoples of Indonesia, such as
the Ngadju of Borneo. Among the latter, for instance, we find the
cosmic directions consist of upriver *(ngadu)*, downriver *(ngawa)*,
sunrise *(kabaloman andau)* and sunset *(kabelapanandau)*,
and their intersection marks the focal point of the cosmos or the
village.[51] The basic concepts expressed in the Nias village plan
are, therefore, presumably older than anything that could be
ascribed to Indian influence. This suggests that we should look
instead to the pre-Indian, Bronze-Iron Age culture of Indonesia
—the Dongson culture—for the origins of Nias cosmology and its
planning system.

One way to test this hypothesis in regard to village planning
is to look at the traditional plans of highland Bali, an area still
largely pre-Hinduistic in culture despite some obvious debts to
India. The schematic plan of a Bali Aga, or original, non-Hinduized
Bali, village, as reconstructed by Roger Tan (Fig. 43), is axial;[52]
upstream *(kaja)* is opposed by downstream *(kelod)* which is
toward the sea (or north in North Bali). At the upper end of the
village is situated the "naval temple" *(pura puseh)* associated with the origins of the village and the sacred house where
village elders assemble *(pura bali agung)*. The two groups of
dwellings (*sibak kangin*, right, and *sibak kaun*, left) are occupied by the two moieties and face one another on the side. Near
the entrance to the village is the temple of the underworld *(pura
dalem)*. The right-hand moiety takes charge of the upper world
temple; the left-hand one conducts funeral rites and ceremonies having to do with the dead. Elders of the two moieties sit
across from one another in the *bale agung* or in two such meetinghouses placed side by side.

In actuality, no Bali Aga village exhibits all of the features
which Tan considers to be ancient.[53] The closest approximation,
that seen at Madenan, consists of two facing rows of houses
with a street between ending at the entrance to the *bale agung*.
Each moiety has its own sanctuary at the head of the row of
dwellings. Another Bali Aga village, Tenganan, departs from
the model still further, placing all the public structures in a row
on the right, running parallel to the line of domestic buildings
(Fig. 44). At the upriver end of the row of public structures is the
wantilan, a building used for cockfights; what appears to be
a lateral cross street intersects the main axis at this point. Still

further upstream is an open place called *para*, or sanctuary, which is also the bathing place. It is important to note that while public meetinghouses at Tenganan are aligned with respect to the upriver-downriver axis, public granaries are oriented cross-axis, probably to conform to the sunrise-sunset (i.e., fertility) line.[54] Bali Aga villages, unlike those elsewhere in Bali, do not make extensive use of compound walls; rather, the entire village is enframed by a wall or hedge known as *kuta*.

The Bali Aga plan contrasts markedly with that of Indianized Balinese villages but closely resembles that of Nias and other non-Hinduized peoples throughout Southeast Asia (Fig. 45). Indian and Chinese planning lie outside the scope of this volume, but both adhere to the macrocosmic-microcosmic principle of crossing cardinal axes. Probably first enunciated in the ancient Near East, this astrological or cosmological system of town planning attempts in its designs to imitate the presumed structure of the universe.[55] Under the influence of the Indian system, the central palace or religious structure became synonymous with the sacred world mountain, Mount Meru in Buddhism and Brahmanism; the name for temple among Indianized Balinese, it should be noted, is Meru. Both the concept and the terminology are lacking in Bali Aga villages. This encourages the view that the planning system employed in old Balinese villages is indeed pre-Indic in origin and therefore also probably an expression of the Dongson culture as seen in Nias, South Borneo, and other traditional areas in Indonesia.

YORUBA, NIGERIA

The peoples of sub-Saharan Africa, with the exception of groups influenced by Islamic or European patterns, traditionally lived either in isolated homesteads or in small villages. Those in arid areas whose lives revolved around cattle herding, particularly in eastern and southern Africa but also in the west African savannah areas, tended to occupy small compounds in the middle of grazing lands (Figs. 46–54); their clustered dwellings seldom formed anything larger than a hamlet.[56] Small villages, on the other hand, have long been characteristic of agricultural peoples dwelling in the humid area extending from the Guinea coast through the Congo basin, where the tsetse fly made cattle raising all but impossible. Here life was based on the cultivation of garden crops, and security from raiders was a paramount consideration (Figs. 55–57).[57] The advent of the slave trade increased this need while also creating new sources of wealth for the heads of petty African states. As a result, African coastal entrepôts and secure inland towns, such as Benin (Figs. 58–60) and Abomey, rapidly increased in population while many of the weaker hinterland areas became virtually depopulated. Thus throughout the western coastal areas of Africa, towns and villages organized on kinship lines had come into being long before the suppression of the slave trade in the late nineteenth century.

There arose, by that time, a need for security from the terrible tribal wars due largely to European interventions in many parts of Africa. In the subsequent colonial era, the governmental preference for dealing with centralized authority intensified the movement toward living in large groups (Figs. 61–62). The most elaborate development toward urbanism in pre-colonial Africa took place among the Yoruba of western Nigeria and Dahomey (see Map A). In 1856 Bowen estimated the populations respectively of Ibadan at 70,000, Lagos 20,000, Ogbomosho 25,000, Iwo 20,000, Abeokuta 60,000, Oyo 25,000, Iseyin 20,000, Ede 20,000, and Ilorin 70,000; the pre-nineteenth-century population totals have been placed at between 5,000 and 30,000.[58] The latter figures are only a guess, since early records are all but non-existent. But they do indicate that many Yoruba were already living in towns when the majority of Africans still resided in homesteads or villages. Hence, while slaving may have accelerated a tendency toward town-dwelling among the Yoruba, it does not account completely for their settlement preferences.

The population density of Yoruba towns also raises the question whether or not these should really be called cities. One may differentiate between towns and cities by means of economic, socio-political, or other criteria.[59] Some scholars, for example, define the city in terms of its economic diversification, particularly the preponderance of a non-agrarian way of life[60]. By this standard the Yoruba metropolitan centers must be classified as towns rather than cities because the majority of the residents continued to venture forth daily to work in their fields. On the other hand, some scholars may place emphasis on the presence of such economic institutions as markets and of technological skills lacking in the countryside. Weaving, sewing, dyeing, wood- and leather-working, blacksmithing, silver-working, and brass smithing were concentrated in Yoruba towns among certain family groups; large-scale regional markets were held there every four or eight days. This pattern certainly points in the direction of urbanism. As regards socio-political criteria, Yoruba centers at first glance give every appearance of urbanization, including hieratic leadership, a military establishment, and religious specialization. It is only when one looks closely at Yoruba socio-political structure that one sees how this system differs from that prevailing in actual cities.

Yoruba towns are structured around the office of divine kingship to which a member of the royal lineage is elected by the "kingmakers" of the other lineages.[61] The divine king, or Oba, of each town embodies in his person the well-being of his community and acts as custodian of the rituals, shrines, and wealth entrusted to his office. The king traces his descent from the legendary Oduduwa, who on orders from the Supreme Being Olodumare, descended to earth at Ile-Ife and inaugurated the first kingship. Though a divine being after his installation, the Yoruba king is not likely to be a tyrant, since his power is counterbalanced by that of a council of elders who can cause him to be deposed or executed for malperformance. Other male members of the royal lineage, though eligible to be elected king, do not normally share in the wealth or prestige of the office; nor can a son ordinarily succeed his father. In other words, the Yoruba system of kingship explicitly functions to prevent the formation of an hereditary urban elite. Hence by this standard too, Yoruba towns cannot really be described as cities.

As is true in the other communities we have discussed, kinship is central to Yoruba economic, religious, and social activities. Traditionally a young Yoruba man had to work for his father until he was thirty years of age, and until then he was almost totally dependent on the family for his training, bride price, and other essentials. Even today it is still possible to see a hundred or so Yoruba men, of all ages but closely related by blood ties, working side by side at the family craft, be it woodcarving, weaving, or brass casting. The countless festivals, priests, and shrines necessary to traditional Yoruba religion also draw their clientele and support from the lineage system. The social cohesion of the lineage is fundamental to the existence and continued growth of Yoruba town life. Indeed, as Bascom puts it: "There is no evidence that city [town] life tended to weaken the kinship bonds or the lineage structure or to produce the increased mobility, instability, and insecurity which Louis Wirth viewed as the result of the social heterogeneity of industrial city life. Although these effects are to be seen at the present time, their causes lie in various features of the acculturative situation ... the Yoruba cities [towns] were based on the kinship bonds as formalized through the lineage system."[62]

The typical residential pattern developed in Yoruba towns consists of a localized segment of the lineage living together in a large, square compound having but a single entrance and bounded by mud walls seven feet high; long, galleried rooms front on one another around a courtyard or impluvium. Each compound houses members of a single extended family. The man who can trace his descent most directly from the lineage founder is the headman of the compound and around him cluster his wives, children, his brothers, their wives and children. At his death, leadership passes to his brother or son, depending on the system in vogue in that particular lineage. The residential group also constitutes a model for the Yoruba religious pantheon. The gods and goddesses, as the Yoruba envision them, are strikingly human, resembling wealthy lineage chiefs or kings and powerful women of the community.

Yoruba town planning is among the most elaborate in Africa south of the Sahara. According to an excellent nineteenth-century source, the town of Ilesha (Figs. 63–64) was deliberately laid out on the pattern of Old Oyo, the second most important center in Yoruba territory.[63] Unfortunately Old Oyo is no longer available for study, having been conquered by the Muslim Fulani peoples in 1837; but the plan of Ilesha still bears a striking resemblance to those of Oyo (Figs. 65–66), Owo (Fig. 67),

Ile-Ife (Fig. 68) and Ado-Ekiti (Fig. 69). Indeed, "there is a growing body of evidence to show that the founders of these new towns [those deriving from Old Oyo] reproduced not only the social and political institutions of their parent towns but also their physical plan... Already, a good number of the towns so far studied show distinctive similarities in their layout."[64]

Examination of all these town plans reveals some of the principles of the Yoruba layout. The form is essentially radial, with intricate subdivisions between the main highways. Three to six principal roads, thirty feet or more wide, lead to adjacent market towns but are important also as processional avenues for innumerable religious groups. The main highways converge into three arteries that meet approximately at right angles in front of the king's palace grounds. The latter precincts are often walled—those at Ife are eighteen feet high and three feet thick at their base—and encompass a large area of up to a square mile.[65] The palace with its grounds is situated in the approximate center of the town but has no particular orientation other than its relation to the arterial roads.

In shape the traditional Yoruba town seems to have been roughly circular. Town walls, although perhaps augmented during the nineteenth-century wars, were evidently an ancient feature, as they figure prominently in the story of King Shango and in military affairs as far south as Ijebu Ode. The circumscribed area was not completely built over, indicating that siege was seldom undertaken against the Yoruba of old. Rather, circumvallation may have served a symbolic purpose, defining by the enclosed space the jurisdiction of the Oba, just as the outer compound wall marked the limit of the headman's authority. For if the development of compounds may be characterized as inward-focusing, the same principle is evident in the layout of the Yoruba town as a whole. Although some tendency toward ribbon development along arteries may be observed, the general pattern is one of nestling together into "quarters," which in turn are sited in relation to main streets or the king's own grounds (Fig. 69). This type of proliferation probably reflects the kinship system, with its tendency toward endless fission, as well as the bonds of allegiance linking each lineage-head to the king.

The Yoruba town plan underscores the social and religious prominence of the institution of kingship. The Yoruba king's palace, which houses his one hundred or so wives, consists of a huge compound that differs from those of ordinary people primarily in the sculptural decoration of the wooden posts that support the galley roofs. This decoration—carved figures in the form of male equestrians and women with babies—not only identifies the king's compound as a privileged structure but also helps to tie together visually architectural units scattered over a distance of several hundred yards. This vast open space is necessary for conducting various ceremonies and rituals in which large numbers of people participate. In other words, given the Yoruba population density and ritual patterns, their town plan had to provide a sizeable civic area, not otherwise engaged, where open-air events having social as well as sacramental functions could take place.

Nor are economic functions neglected. The most important market is frequently set up directly outside the entrance to the palace grounds, where the various highways converge. Although the Obas usually show themselves to the people only on ceremonial occasions, the placement of the market so near the palace seems motivated in part by a desire to regularize market relations. The Yoruba kings recognize the dangers of market transactions, and in many Yoruba towns there is a special "master of the market"—in Oyo the job was once held by a woman—whose task it is to regulate market activities and punish miscreants on behalf of the Oba.

The Yoruba town of Ketu in Dahomey (Fig. 70) differs somewhat in plan from the Nigerian centers discussed above. The population of Ketu, estimated at between 10,000 and 15,000 in the 1850's, lived in a town surrounded by two concentric, sixteen-foot-high stone and clay walls having but a single gate that opened toward the north.[66] Two huge wooden doors, said to close themselves magically in time of danger, barred the way at night. Ketu was divided schematically into two halves (right, or west, and left or east) with respect to an imaginary central line running directly south from this gateway. Unlike the location in other Yoruba towns, the royal palace was situated near the southern wall on the eastern (left-hand) side of this line; the royal compound was set off by a roughly rectangular wall having three adjacent entrances on the north, the left and right of which were reserved for the king's exclusive use. The queen's house was situated to the south of the king's. A large market met outside the walls, but a small one was held near the center of town. This plan, with its very high walls and few entrances, may reflect the military insecurity of Ketu, which was conquered time and again in the nineteenth century. But many features of the plan appear to be consistent with traditional Yoruba town lay-out in Nigeria.

One of the least explored yet potentially most interesting aspects of the Yoruba town plan is its relation to cosmology and geomancy. The axial north-south orientation of the Ketu town brings to mind the installation ritual of the Ketu king who, at the time of his coronation, visited four special houses situated respectively north, west, east, and south of the village.[67] This custom of circumambulation, whereby the king takes symbolic possession of his dominions, is found in many parts of the world and is particularly characteristic of kingship in the ancient Near East. Many other Nigerian traits, including the custom of linking the cardinal directions with different colors and deities, the system of divination, fish-legged figures, the "animal master" theme, bird-serpent combats as royal symbols, the snake that bites its own tail, and so on, have been ascribed to influences stemming ultimately from the pre-Islamic Near East, although possibly not reaching Nigeria until the middle of the first millennium A.D.[68] All of this makes it likely that Yoruba urbanism and town layout are related ultimately to Near Eastern concepts, although the precise source of this influence and the avenues by which it reached Nigeria are as yet uncertain.

CONCLUSIONS

The foregoing case studies, for all the arbitrariness of their selection, clearly underline certain basic truths about planning in the primitive world. In every instance that we have seen, social relationships rather than geometric order appear to be the major determinant in the placement of buildings. This would be equally true had we chosen to examine other villages or cultures having completely irregular layouts. Such an analysis, however, is more appropriate to an anthropological study than to a volume on town planning. Nevertheless, by isolating orderly examples, we have demonstrated for the non-specialist the existence of *planning*, as opposed merely to plans, in the primitive world.

The examples also indicate a correlation between the level of economic development and the complexity of planning schemes evolved. The simplest societies, such as those of the Pygmies and Bushmen, retain a maximum of design flexibility, just as their economic and social systems insist upon physical mobility and relatively free interpersonal relationships. The more sedentary groups become, the greater their emphasis on land and property and the more inclined they are toward fixed spatial organization. In still more complex groups, an economic surplus combined with increasingly hieratic social and political distinctions frequently prompts the privileged placement of meetinghouse, market place, or important chief's dwelling. Social and religious sanctions are necessary if such developments are to take place; but without an economic base they could scarcely have any real reason for being.

Religious concepts also play a profound part in planning in the primitive world, but their role is often difficult to categorize. Such radically different cultures as the Bushmen, the Cheyenne, and the Nias Islanders independently identified the east with the renewal of life. The same idea appears among the cattle-herding Herero of southwestern Africa, whose sacred fire is always located in the easternmost hut of the circle that forms their *kraal*.[69] The concept of the center is also widespread, finding expression in Haida, Mailu, Nias, and Yoruba as well as many other areas. The Pueblo Indians' sacred ceremonial structure, the *kiva*, for example, is often centrally located. Feasts and celebrations were held in the center of Indian villages in North Carolina (Fig. 71), on the Great Plains, and in South America (Figs. 72–73). In Dongson-influenced eastern Flores, Indonesia, families having houses in the center of the village are called the "mast" and "sail" and are believed to be descended from the original ancestors who arrived long ago in Flores by ship.[70] The link between ship, ancestor, and center is also observed in many other conservative areas in Indonesia.

Military and political factors apparently gain importance in the primitive world with the growth in wealth and prestige of individual centers. Defense against enemies was a primary consideration in the villages in west Africa, and they were formerly protected by palisades or hedges. The same is true in such diverse areas as central and eastern Africa, Indonesia, New Guinea, New Zealand (Fig. 75), the Northwest Coast of America, and Florida (Fig. 76). Defensive siting, however, may involve religious concepts as much as practical considerations; the mountain villages in Sumba are often located miles away from water on sites hallowed by custom (Fig. 77). On the other hand, the Onondaga of New York (Fig. 78) developed a system of water storage with ponds and gutters to put out fires within their thirty-foot-high palisaded village.[71]

There is, in other words, no such thing as a "primitive approach to planning" even in matters so fundamental as defense. Each society has worked out a solution that is appropriate to and in harmony with its own particular circumstances, and in so doing each has achieved something worthy of recognition.

MACABO

COFFEE

HUTS

LOCATION OF CEREMONIES
OF EXCISION AND CIRCUMCISION

VARIED CULTIVATION

SACRED WOODS

MANUFACTURE OF
PARPENS OF POTO-POTO

THE FAVORITES

COMMUNITY HUT

COMMUNITY HUTS

SMALL RIVER

SERVANT

HEADMAN'S HOUSE

KING'S
PLAZA

COMMUNITY HUT

VISITOR'S QUARTER

DOOR

WIVES

GARAGE

WIVES

ALL RIVER

GUARD

WASHING HOUSE

ANCESTRAL SKULLS

ANCESTOR'S STATUES

COMMUNITY HUT

BANANA TREES

MAIN MARKETPLACE

SIGNAL STATION

20 30 40 50 60 70 80 90 100   METERS

ENTRANCE

2. Model of Batoufam village. Bamileke, Cameroun, Africa.

3. View of Dogon village from Bandiagara Escarpment. Mali, Africa.
4. Ideal schema of a Dogon village. Mali, Africa.

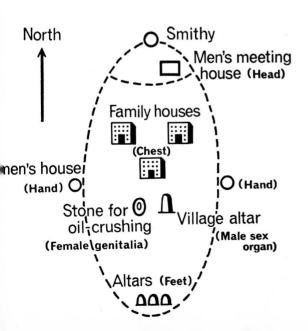

North

Smithy

Men's meeting house (Head)

Family houses

(Chest)

men's house (Hand)

(Hand)

Stone for oil-crushing

(Female genitalia)

Village altar

(Male sex organ)

Altars (Feet)

5. Cliff Palace. Mesa Verde National Park, Colorado.
6. Plan of Cliff Palace. Mesa Verde National Park, Colorado. The circular chambers were *kivas* or ceremonial centers, the rectangular structures living quarters and storerooms.

CLIFF PALACE
MESA VERDE NATIONAL PARK
COLORADO

1 STORY   2 STORY   3 STORY   4 STORY

7. Reconstruction of Pueblo Bonito. Chaco Canyon National Monument, New Mexico.
8. Ground plan of Pueblo Bonito. Chaco Canyon National Monument, New Mexico. As in the Cliff Palace (Fig. 6), the circular chambers were *kivas*, the rectangular structures living quarters and storerooms.

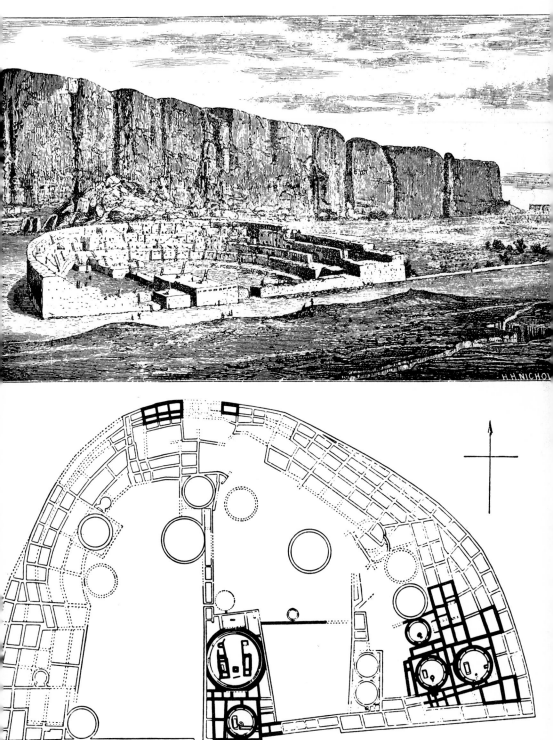

LARGE STONE

SCALE OF FEET

9. Aerial view of Oraibi village. Hopi, Arizona.
10. Plan of Oraibi village. Hopi, Arizona.

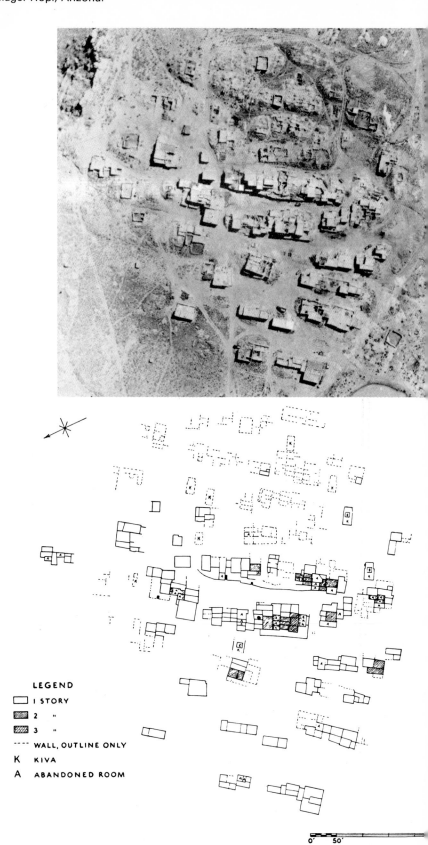

LEGEND

☐ I STORY

▨ 2 "

▨ 3 "

---- WALL, OUTLINE ONLY

K KIVA

A ABANDONED ROOM

0'   50'

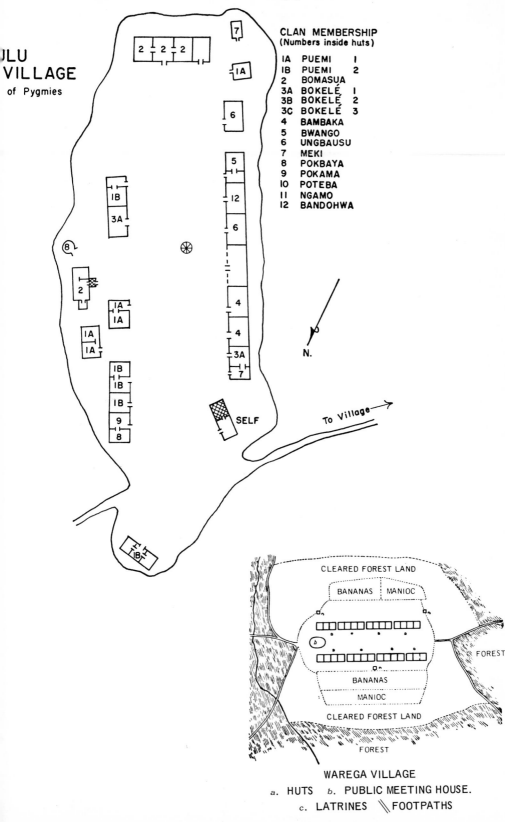

11. Plan of Mbuti Pygmy camp in Epulu village.
Ituri Forest, northeastern Congo, Africa.
12. Plan of Lega (Warega) village. Northeastern
Congo, Africa.

JLU
VILLAGE
of Pygmies

CLAN MEMBERSHIP
(Numbers inside huts)

IA PUEMI   I
IB PUEMI   2
2   BOMASUA
3A BOKELÉ   I
3B BOKELÉ   2
3C BOKELÉ   3
4   BAMBAKA
5   BWANGO
6   UNGBAUSU
7   MEKI
8   POKBAYA
9   POKAMA
IO POTEBA
II NGAMO
12 BANDOHWA

N.

SELF

To Village

CLEARED FOREST LAND

BANANAS   MANIOC

FOREST

BANANAS

MANIOC

CLEARED FOREST LAND

FOREST

WAREGA VILLAGE
a. HUTS   b. PUBLIC MEETING HOUSE.
c. LATRINES   \\ FOOTPATHS

13. Plan of Mbuti Pygmy huts. Camp on Lelo River (Apa Lelo), Ituri Forest, northeastern Congo.
14. Plan of Mbuti Pygmy huts. Camp on Lelo River (Apa Lelo), Ituri Forest, northeastern Congo.

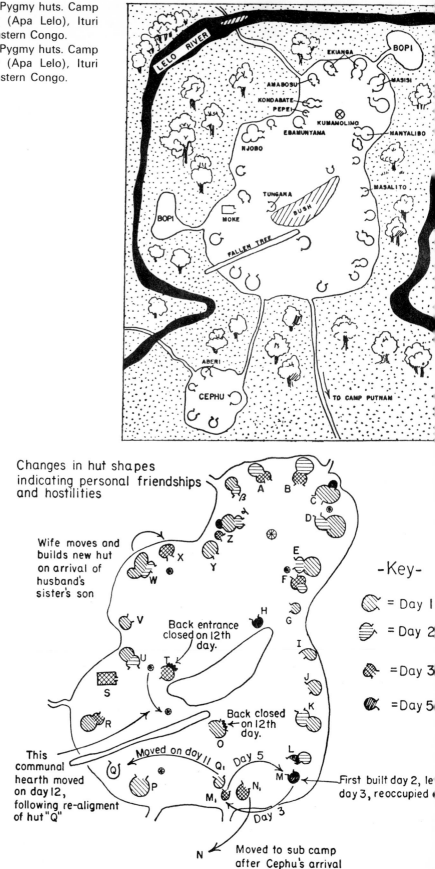

Changes in hut shapes indicating personal friendships and hostilities

Wife moves and builds new hut on arrival of husband's sister's son

Back entrance closed on 12th day.

This communal hearth moved on day 12, following re-aligment of hut "Q"

Moved on day 11

Day 5

Back closed on 12th day.

First built day 2, le day 3, reoccupied

Moved to sub camp after Cephu's arrival

-Key-

= Day 1

= Day 2

= Day 3

= Day 5

Bushman Settlement
(after Backhouse)

Walton 1954

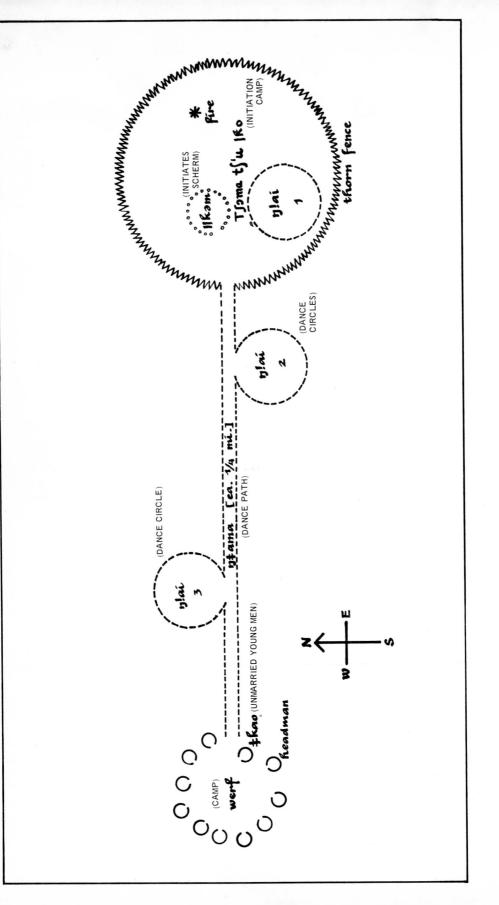

(INITIATION CAMP)

Tʃɔma tʃ'u !Ko

*fire

(INITIATES SCHERM)
||Kam·

ɳ!ai 1

thorn fence

(DANCE CIRCLES)

ɳ!ai 2

ɳtana [ca. ¼ mi.]
(DANCE PATH)

(DANCE CIRCLE)

ɳ!ai 3

‡Kao (UNMARRIED YOUNG MEN)

headman

(CAMP)
werf

N
W ─┼─ E
S

16. Plan of Bushman werf, Kalahari Desert, Africa.

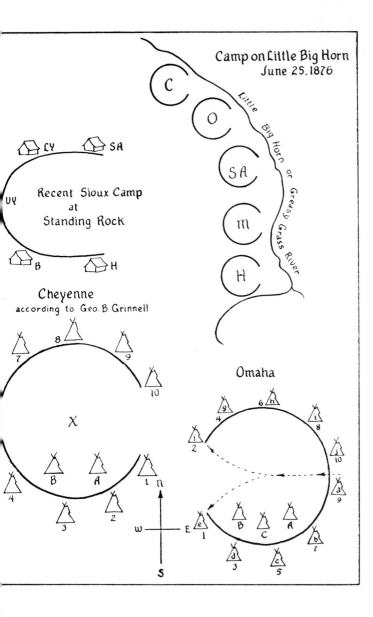

Camp on Little Big Horn
June 25. 1876

Little Big Horn or Greasy Grass River

Recent Sioux Camp
at
Standing Rock

Cheyenne
according to Geo. B. Grinnell

Omaha

20. Plan of ancient Cheyenne camp circle.
    Western Plains, United States.

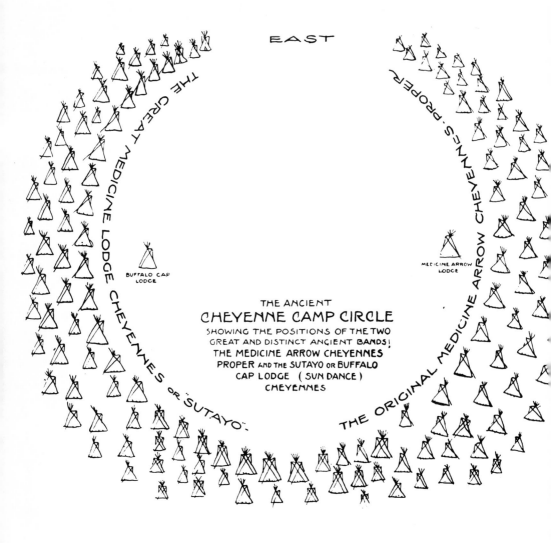

EAST

THE GREAT MEDICINE LODGE CHEYENNES or "SUTAYO"

THE ORIGINAL MEDICINE ARROW CHEYENNES-PROPER

BUFFALO CAP
LODGE

MEDICINE ARROW
LODGE

THE ANCIENT
CHEYENNE CAMP CIRCLE
SHOWING THE POSITIONS OF THE TWO
GREAT AND DISTINCT ANCIENT BANDS;
THE MEDICINE ARROW CHEYENNES
PROPER AND THE SUTAYO OR BUFFALO
CAP LODGE (SUN DANCE)
CHEYENNES

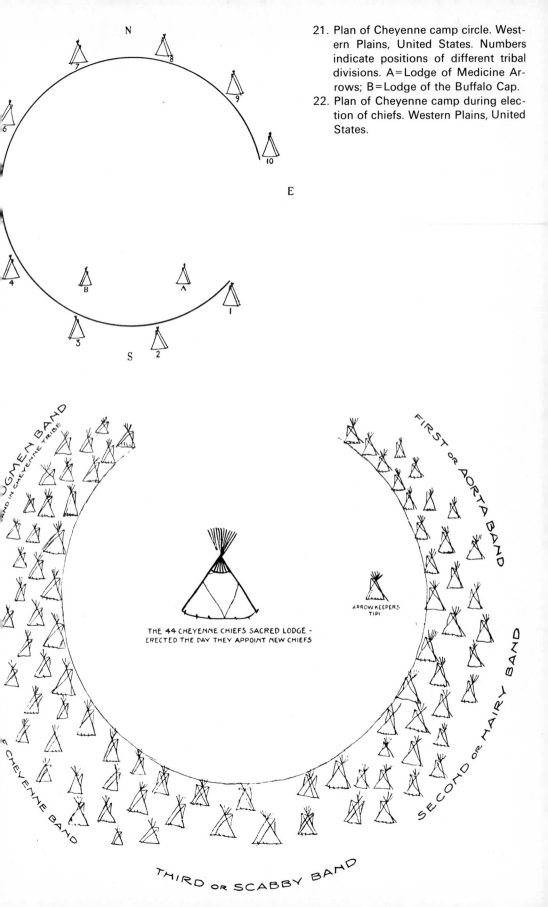

N

7

8

9

10

E

6

4

B

A

1

3

2

S

21. Plan of Cheyenne camp circle. Western Plains, United States. Numbers indicate positions of different tribal divisions. A=Lodge of Medicine Arrows; B=Lodge of the Buffalo Cap.
22. Plan of Cheyenne camp during election of chiefs. Western Plains, United States.

UGMEN BAND
AND IN CHEYENNE TRIBE

FIRST OR AORTA BAND

ARROW KEEPERS TIPI

THE 44 CHEYENNE CHIEFS SACRED LODGE - ERECTED THE DAY THEY APPOINT NEW CHIEFS

CHEYENNE BAND

SECOND OR HAIRY BAND

THIRD OR SCABBY BAND

23. Village sites on Anthony Island. Haida, Queen Charlotte Islands, British Columbia, Canada.
24. Second village at Skidegate. Haida. Queen Charlotte Islands, British Columbia, Canada.

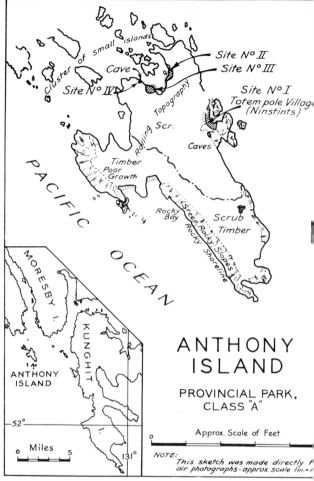

25. Plan of Ninstints village. Haida, Queen Charlotte Islands, British Columbia, Canada.

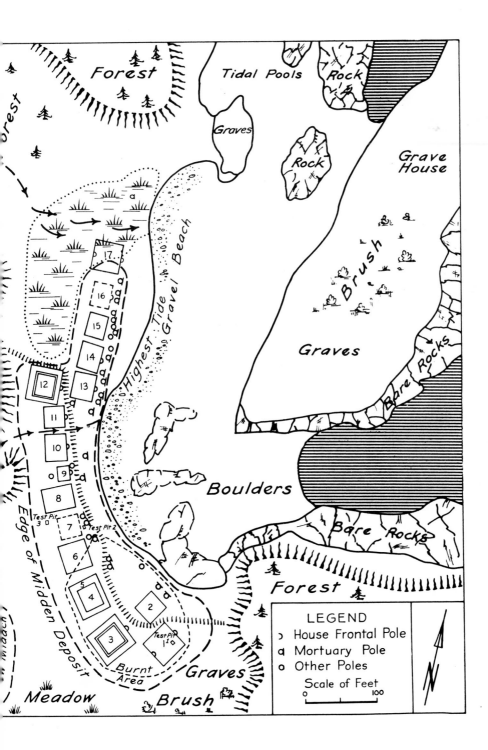

Forest

Tidal Pools

Rock

Graves

Rock

Grave House

Forest

Brush

Highest Tide Gravel Beach

17

16

15

14

12 13

11

10

9

8

Test Pit 3

7

Test Pit 2

6

5

4

2

3

Test Pit 1

Graves

Bare Rocks

Boulders

Bare Rocks

Forest

Edge of Midden Deposit

Burnt Area

Meadow

Graves

Brush

LEGEND
House Frontal Pole
Mortuary Pole
Other Poles
Scale of Feet
0   100

N

26 and 27. Mailu Island village. Papua, New Guinea.

28. Plan showing the disposition of the four village clans and their subdivisions. Mailu Island village, Papua, New Guinea.

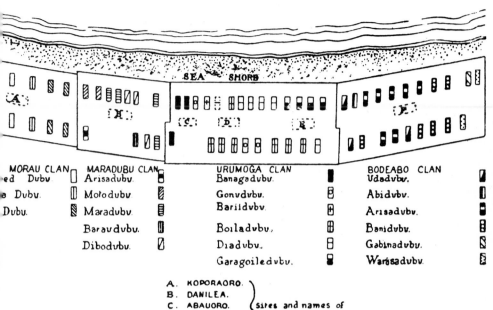

MORAU CLAN		MARADUBU CLAN		URUMOGA CLAN		BODEABO CLAN	
ed Dubu.	🞒	Arisadubu.	▣	Banagadubu.	▮	Udadubu.	▨
a Dubu.	▥	Molodubu	▦	Gonudubu.	⊟	Abidubu.	▯
Dubu.	▤	Maradubu.	▤	Bariidubu	⊞	Arisadubu.	▤
		Baraudubu.	▨	Boiladubu,	⊞	Banidubu.	▤
		Dibodubu.	▧	Diadubu.	⊟	Gabinadubu.	▨
				Garagoiledubu.	▮	Warasadubu.	▤

A. KOPORAORO.
B. DANILEA.
C. ABAUORO. { sites and names of
D. ONIBUORO.   vanished Club Houses.
E. DARIAVARA.
F. GOISEORO.

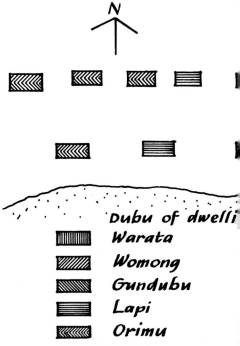

N

Dubu of dwelli

Warata

Womong

Gundubu

Lapi

Orimu

29. Mailu Island village street. Papua, New Guinea.
30. Street with clubhouse. Möu village, Roro, Papua, New Guinea.
31. Plan of Boru village. Baxter Bay, Papua, New Guinea.

C - L.M.S. Church
M - Mission teacher's dwelling
T - Trader's house

33. Village in mangrove swamp. Marshalls Lagoon, Papua, New Guinea.

34. Plan of Omarakana village. Kiriwina district, Trobriand Islands, New Guinea.
35. Yam houses. Kiriwina district, Trobriand Islands, New Guinea.

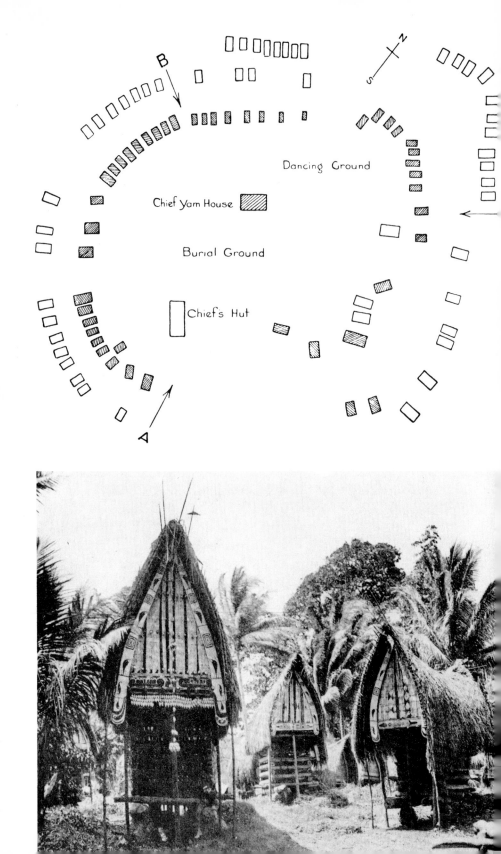

Dancing Ground

Chief Yam House

Burial Ground

Chief's Hut

36. Karo Batak village. Sumatra, Indonesia.
37. Schematic plan of a Karo Batak village. Sumatra, Indonesia.

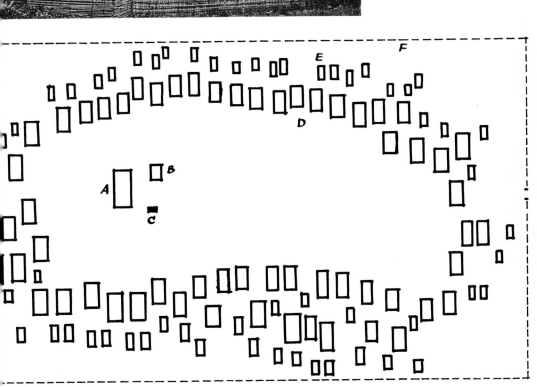

ARO BATAK VILLAGE

djambur : upper - rice barn
           lower - meetings, reception of guests, etc.
geriten : charnel house
rice stamping block
- dwellings
- private rice barns
- remnants of old stronghold

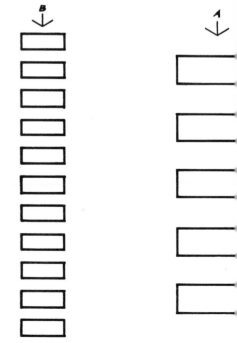

38. Toradja Sa'dan village. Central Celebes, Indonesia.
39. Schematic plan of a Toradja Sa'dan village. Central Celebes, Indonesia.

TORADJA SA'DAN VILLAGE
A - dwellings
B - rice barns

41. Schematic plan of Bawamataluö village, South Nias, Indonesia.

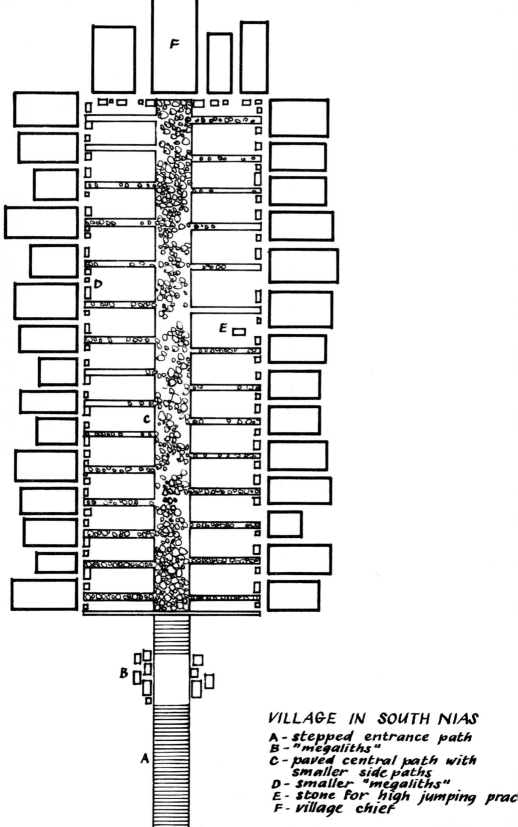

VILLAGE IN SOUTH NIAS
A - stepped entrance path
B - "megaliths"
C - paved central path with
    smaller side paths
D - smaller "megaliths"
E - stone for high jumping prac
F - village chief

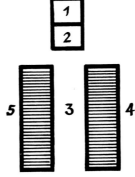

temple of origin of village

(sacred) building for assembly of village elders

village space

group of dwellings (right moiety)

group of dwellings (left moiety)

infernal temple

44. Schematic plan of Tenganan village. Bali, Indonesia.

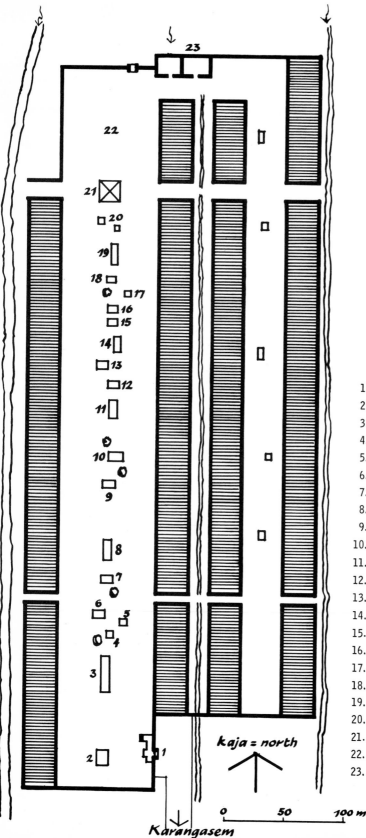

1. main entrance
2. infernal temple
3. assembly building
4. household temple
5. shrine
6. signal block tower
7. rice granary
8. youngmen's building
9. rice granary
10. shrine
11. girl's building
12. rice granary
13. shrine
14. men's building
15. storage
16. rice granary
17. shrine
18. rice granary
19. women's building
20. temporary buildings
21. cockfight building
22. empty space called pura (temple)
23. bathing place

23

22

21
20
19
18
17
16
15
14
13
12
11
10
9
8
7
6
5
4
3
2 1

kaja = north

0   50   100 m

Karangasem

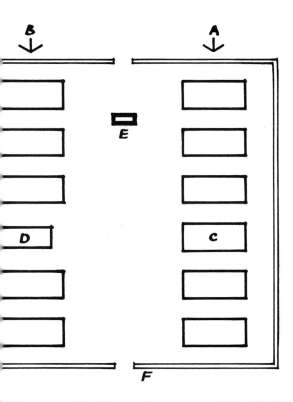

B
A
E
D
C
F

BA BATAK VILLAGE ON SAMOSIR
ons + families
daughters + families
village chief
opo = rice barn
imin = stone charnel case
ence on small dike

46. Plan of chief's village, "At the Place of Rumours." Swaziland, South Africa.

Ekuhhetsheni—At the Place of Rumours, Village of a Chief. A, Cattle byre (square, and of stone). B, Calf byre. C, Pig-sty. 1, Enclosure of wife and her small son (2 years old). (a) Living hut. (b) Store or kitchen. 2, Enclosure of wife, two daughters (10 years, 6 years) and son (3 years). (a), (b). 3, Enclosure of wife, 2 sons (8 years, 5 years) and daughter (2 years). (a), (b). 4, Main enclosure. Senior wife, acting as " mother," one daughter (18 years). (a1), Living hut of mother. (a2) Separate hut of daughter. (b) Store huts. (c) Special store huts attached to great hut. In them are kept grain from headman's main fields. 5, Enclosure of wife, her grown daughter with young baby. (a1) Living hut of mother. (a2) Living hut of daughter. No lobola has been paid and she and her baby are staying at her parents'. (b) Store huts and kitchen. 6, Rondavels built for the chief. It is an innovation for the headman to have such private quarters. 7, Enclosure of wife, two daughters (8 and 5 years old) and son (12 years). 8, Barracks of men, occupied at night by adolescent and unmarried sons.

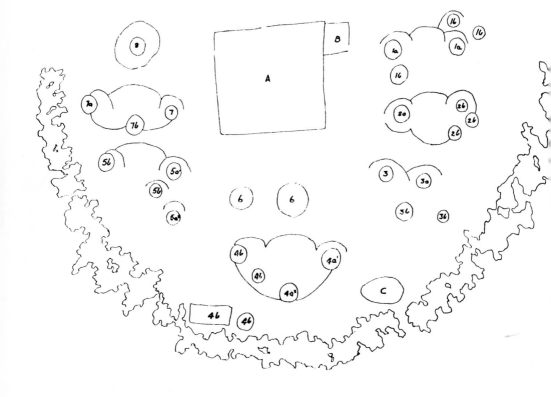

48. Zulu *kraal*. South Africa.

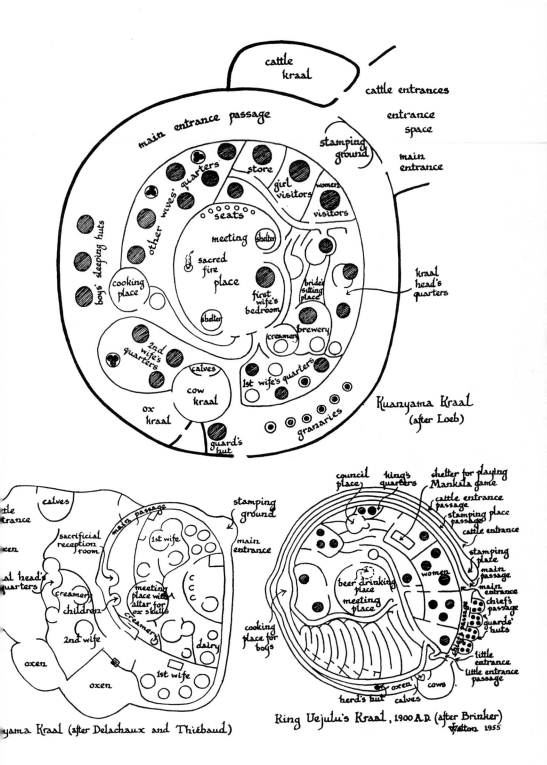

Kuanyama Kraal
(after Loeb)

yama Kraal (after Delachaux and Thiébaud)

King Uejulu's Kraal, 1900 A.D. (after Brinker)
Walton 1955

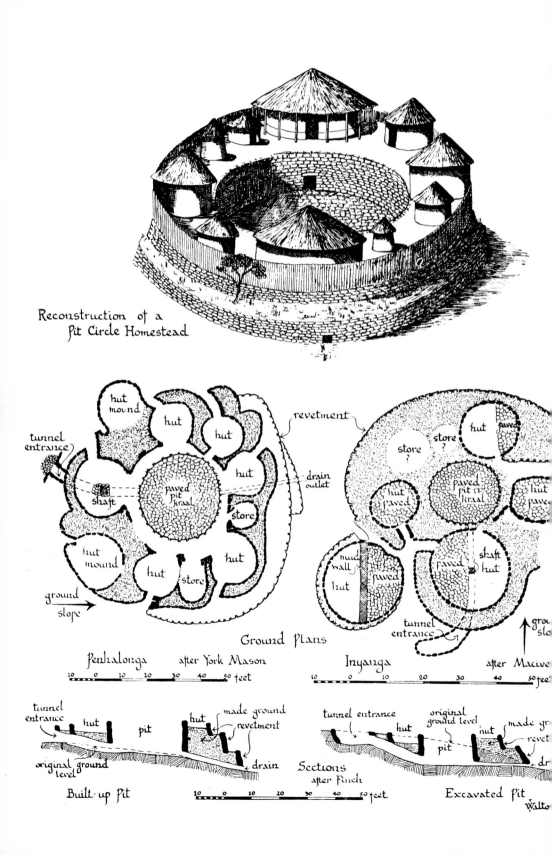

Reconstruction of a
Pit Circle Homestead

hut mound

hut

hut

tunnel entrance

shaft

paved Pit Kraal

hut

store

hut mound

hut

store

hut

revetment

drain outlet

store ?

store ?

hut

paved

paved Pit Kraal

hut paved

hut paved

mud wall

hut

paved

paved

shaft hut

tunnel entrance

ground slope

ground slope

Ground Plans

Penhalonga   after York Mason
10   0   10   20   30   40   50 feet

Inyanga   after Macive
10   0   10   20   30   40   50 fee

tunnel entrance

hut

pit

hut

made ground

revetment

original ground level

drain

Built-up Pit

tunnel entrance

hut

original ground level

hut

made gr

revet

pit

dr

Sections
after Finch

Excavated Pit

10   0   10   20   30   40   50 feet

Walto

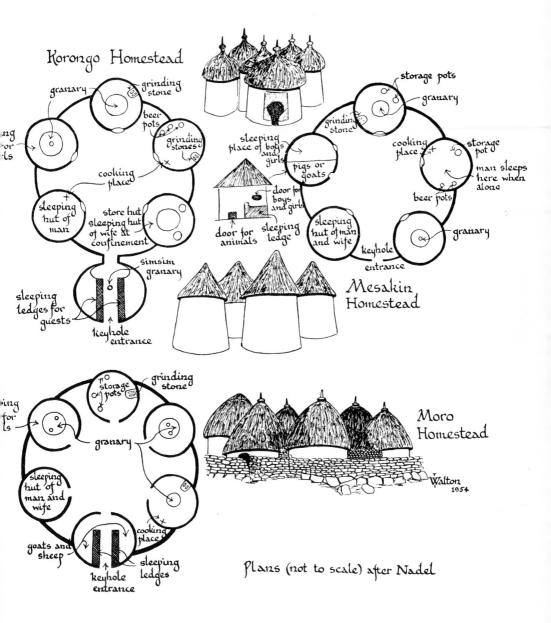

Korongo Homestead

granary
grinding stone
beer pots
grinding stones
cooking place
sleeping hut of man
store hut sleeping hut of wife at confinement
simsim granary
sleeping ledges for guests
keyhole entrance

sleeping place of boys and girls
door for boys and girls
door for animals
sleeping ledge

storage pots
granary
grinding stone
cooking place
storage pot
man sleeps here when alone
beer pots
pigs or goats
sleeping hut of man and wife
keyhole entrance
granary

Mesakin Homestead

storage pots
grinding stone
granary
sleeping hut of man and wife
goats and sheep
keyhole entrance
cooking place
sleeping ledges

Moro Homestead

Walton 1954

Plans (not to scale) after Nadel

52. Plan of Massa homestead. Yagoua, Cameroun, Africa.

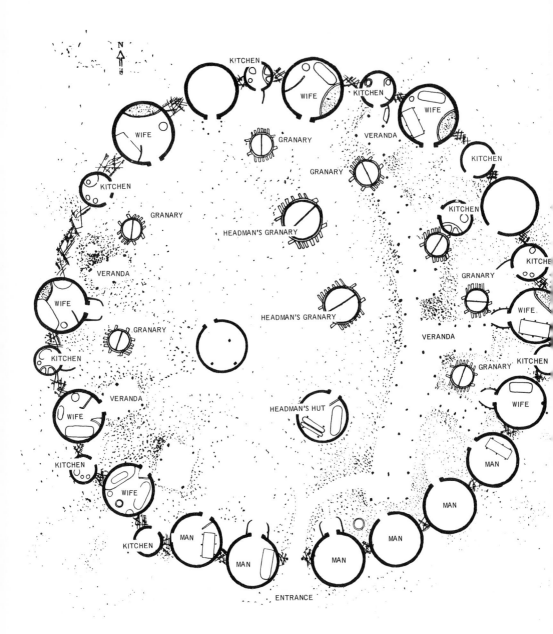

KITCHEN

WIFE

KITCHEN

WIFE

GRANARY

VERANDA

KITCHEN

WIFE

KITCHEN

GRANARY

GRANARY

KITCHEN

KITCHEN

HEADMAN'S GRANARY

GRANARY

VERANDA

WIFE

GRANARY

VERANDA

HEADMAN'S GRANARY

VERANDA

WIFE

GRANARY

KITCHEN

KITCHEN

WIFE

VERANDA

WIFE

HEADMAN'S HUT

MAN

KITCHEN

WIFE

MAN

MAN

KITCHEN

MAN

MAN

MAN

MAN

ENTRANCE

0 1 2 3 4 5 ME

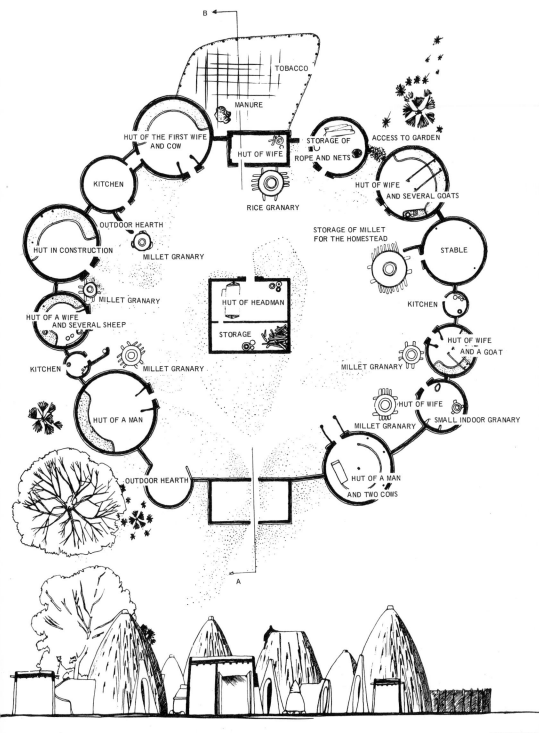

B

TOBACCO

MANURE

HUT OF THE FIRST WIFE
AND COW

HUT OF WIFE

STORAGE OF
ROPE AND NETS

ACCESS TO GARDEN

KITCHEN

HUT OF WIFE
AND SEVERAL GOATS

RICE GRANARY

OUTDOOR HEARTH

STORAGE OF MILLET
FOR THE HOMESTEAD

STABLE

MILLET GRANARY

HUT IN CONSTRUCTION

MILLET GRANARY

HUT OF HEADMAN

KITCHEN

HUT OF A WIFE
AND SEVERAL SHEEP

STORAGE

HUT OF WIFE
AND A GOAT

KITCHEN

MILLET GRANARY

MILLET GRANARY

HUT OF A MAN

HUT OF WIFE

SMALL INDOOR GRANARY

MILLET GRANARY

OUTDOOR HEARTH

HUT OF A MAN
AND TWO COWS

A

ELEVATION AB

0 1 2 3 4 5   10 METERS

54. Plan of Matakam homestead. Cameroun, Africa.

ELEVATION AB

EARTH MOUNDS
SYMBOLIZING FERTILITY

THRESHING-FLOOR
FOR MILLET

TREE WHERE MILLET DRIES

WOOD STORAGE

HUT FOR ASHES

GROUND-NUT GRANARY OF
HEADMAN

HUT OF
YOUNGER SON

BARN

MILLET GRANARY OF
HEADMAN

HUT OF HEADMAN

GOAT STABLE

WATER STORAGE

HUT OF SECOND WIFE
AND SON

MILLET AND GROUND-NUT GRANARY
OF FIRST WIFE

STORAGE OF HEADMAN

HUT OF CALF OF SON

GRANARY OF HEADMAN

MILLET AND GROUND-NUT GRANARY

HUT OF
FIRST WIFE
OF SON

STABLE

GRANARY HUT OF SON

GRINDING AREA FOR MILLET

GRANARY OF WIFE OF SON

KITCHEN

HUT OF
HEADMAN'S OX

HUT
OF WIFE

KITCHEN

GRANARY-HUT

A

MILLET GRANARIES OF HEADMAN

0   1   2   3   4   5   METERS

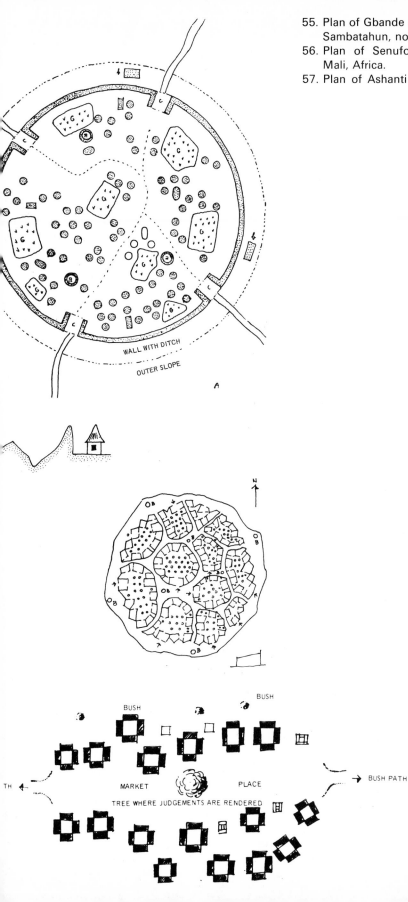

55. Plan of Gbande (Bande), fortified town. Sambatahun, northern Liberia, Africa.
56. Plan of Senufo village near Sikasso. Mali, Africa.
57. Plan of Ashanti hamlet. Ghana, Africa.

WALL WITH DITCH

OUTER SLOPE

A

N

OB

BUSH

BUSH

TH

MARKET

PLACE

BUSH PATH

TREE WHERE JUDGEMENTS ARE RENDERED

A. The house for ye old and young Queens.
B. The yard of ye Royall court.
C. The gate of said court.
D. The Palace of ye Kings court.
E. The Kings progres which hee
      Rideth once a year.
F. His nobles & kindred on horsback.
G. The musicains playing after
      the King.
H. The fools & Dwarfs.
I. The players before ye King &ᵗ
      Tame Leopards.

A. t'Vrouwen timmer of Huys van de Oude
  en Ionge Koninginne.
B. Wal van het Koninglijcke Hof.
C. De Poort des zelven Hofs.
D. Paleisen des Konings Hofs.
E. Staesi hoe de Koning een mael
  SIaers uitrydt.
F. Syn Adel en Bloetvrienden te Paert.
G. Speelders achter den Koning.
H. Gekken en Dwergen.
I. Speelders voor den Koning met
  tamme Tygers.

59. Plan of Benin City and the royal palace. Nigeria, Africa.

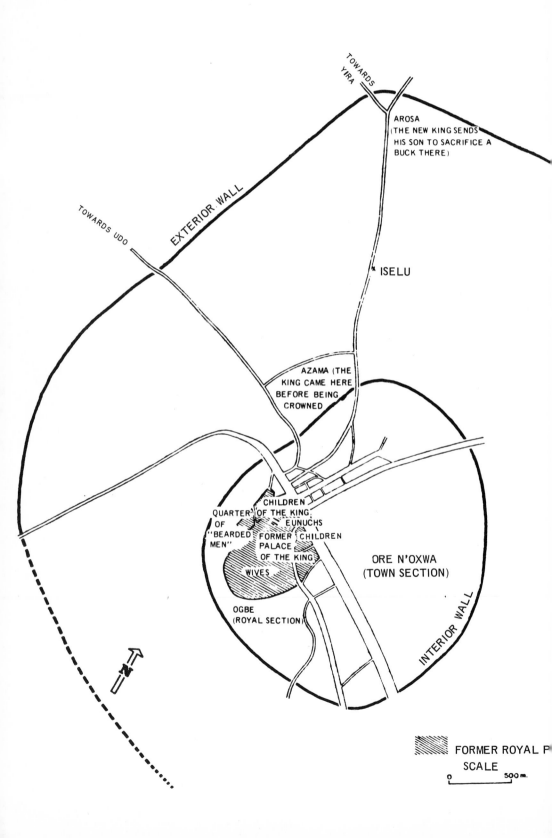

TOWARDS YIRA

AROSA
(THE NEW KING SENDS
HIS SON TO SACRIFICE A
BUCK THERE)

EXTERIOR WALL

TOWARDS UDO

ISELU

AZAMA (THE
KING CAME HERE
BEFORE BEING
CROWNED

CHILDREN
QUARTER OF THE KING
OF   EUNUCHS
"BEARDED   FORMER CHILDREN
MEN"   PALACE
           OF THE KING
       WIVES

ORE N'OXWA
(TOWN SECTION)

OGBE
(ROYAL SECTION)

INTERIOR WALL

N

FORMER ROYAL P

SCALE

0   500 m.

63. Plan of Ilesha showing relation of palace (Afin) to chiefs' compounds. Yoruba, Nigeria, Africa.

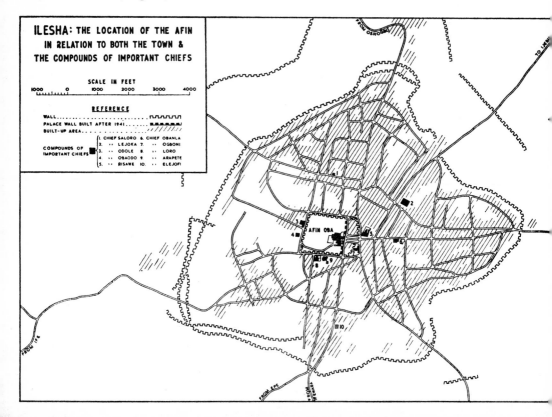

64. Aerial view of Ilesha. Yoruba, Nigeria, Africa.

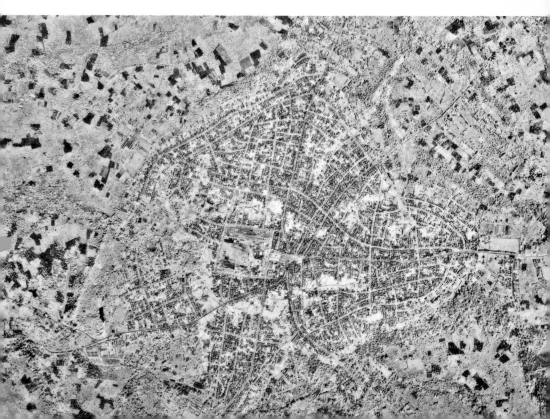

65. Aerial view of Oyo. Yoruba, Nigeria, Africa.

66. Plan of compounds around Afin Oyo (Oyo palace). Yoruba, Nigeria, Africa.

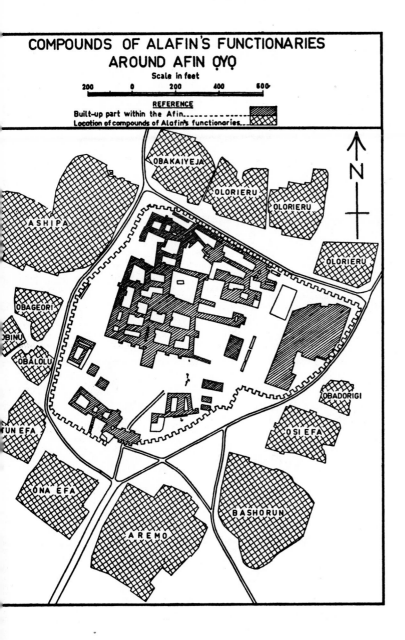

COMPOUNDS OF ALAFIN'S FUNCTIONARIES
AROUND AFIN OYO

Scale in feet

200   0   200   400   600

REFERENCE

Built-up part within the Afin..................
Location of compounds of Alafin's functionaries....

N

67. Plan of Owo. Yoruba, Nigeria, Africa.

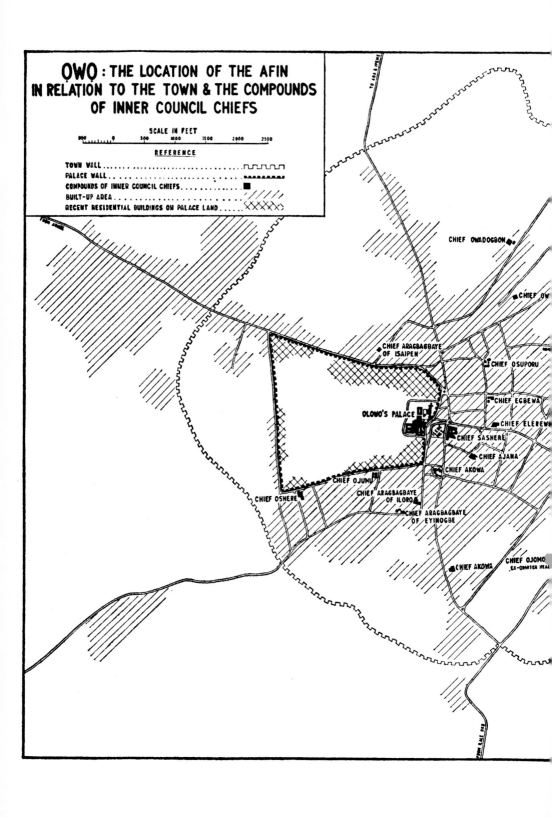

OWO : THE LOCATION OF THE AFIN
IN RELATION TO THE TOWN & THE COMPOUNDS
OF INNER COUNCIL CHIEFS

SCALE IN FEET

REFERENCE

TOWN WALL . . . .
PALACE WALL . . . .
COMPOUNDS OF INNER COUNCIL CHIEFS . . . .
BUILT-UP AREA . . . .
RECENT RESIDENTIAL BUILDINGS ON PALACE LAND . . . . . .

CHIEF OWADOGBON

CHIEF OW

CHIEF ARAGBAGBAYE
OF ISAIPEN

CHIEF OSUPORU

CHIEF EGBEWA

OLOWO'S PALACE

CHIEF ELEREWU

CHIEF SASHERE

CHIEF AJANA

CHIEF AKOWA

CHIEF OJUMU

CHIEF OSHERE

CHIEF ARAGBAGBAYE
OF ILORO

CHIEF ARAGBAGBAYE
OF EYINOGBE

CHIEF AKOWA

CHIEF OJOMO
EX-QUARTER HEAD

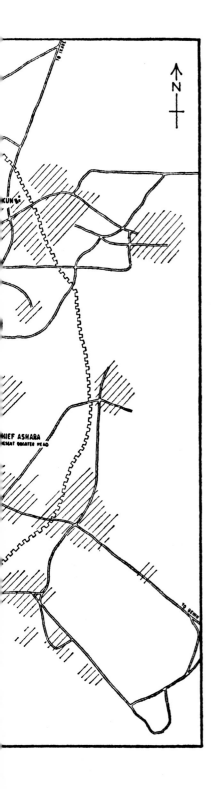

68. Plan of Ile-Ife, Yoruba, Nigeria,
Africa.

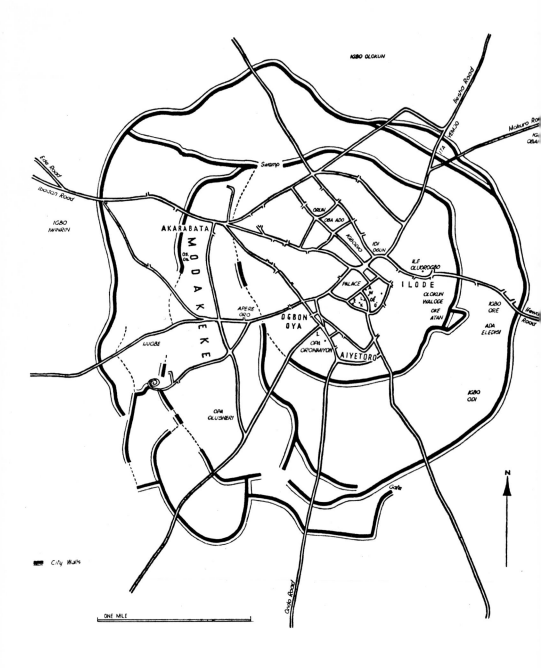

IGBO OLOKUN

Iesha Road

Mokuro Road

IGB
OBA

ITA

YEMOO

Swamp

Ede Road

Ibadan Road

IGBO
IWINRIN

AKARABATA

M
O
D
A
K
E
K
E

OS
OR

ORUN

OBA ADO

IDI
OGUN

KEDODO

ILE
OLUOROGBO

PALACE

ILODE

OLOKUN
WALODE

OKE
ATAN

IGBO
ORE

Howa
Road

ADA
ELEDISI

APERE
ORO

OGBON
OYA

IJUGBE

OPA
ORONMIYON

AIYETORO

IGBO
ODI

OPA
OLUSHERI

Gate

Ondo Road

N

City Walls

ONE MILE

70. Schematic plan of Ketu. Yoruba, Dahomey, Africa.

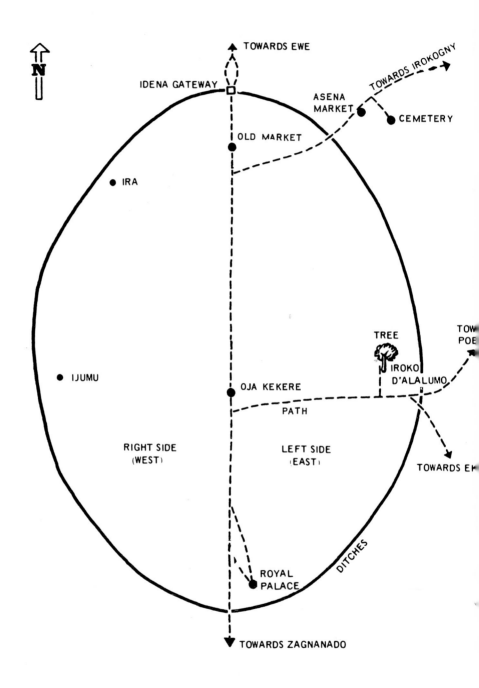

The towne of Pomeiock and true forme of their howses, couered and enclosed some wth matts, and some wth barcks of trees. All compassed abowt wth smale poles stock thick together in stedd of a wall.

8

72. Plan of Bororo village. South central Brazil.
73, Plan of Shavante village. Matto Grosso, central Brazil.

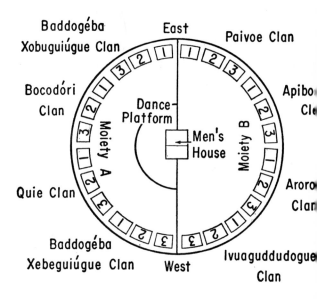

Baddogéba
Xobuguiúgue Clan
East
Paivoe Clan

Bocodóri
Clan

Dance-
Platform

Apibo
Cl

Men's
House

Moiety A

Moiety B

Quie Clan

Aroro
Clan

Baddogéba
Xebeguiúgue Clan
West

Ivuaguddudogue
Clan

74. Plan of Todo village. Manggarai, Flores, Indonesia.
75. Drawing of Maori fortified village. New Zealand.

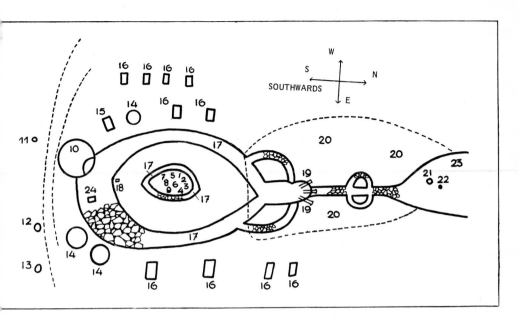

GROUND PLAN OF TODO VILLAGE

 1. – 9. Ancestral Groves
10. The large round dalu-house
11. Kondo rae, the war-stone
12. Liang Paku, the inclined stone
13. Lolo bali, the wedge-shaped stone
14. Round houses
15. The rectangular house of the ruler's mother
16. The other rectangular houses

17. The stone-covered ovals
18. Watu usang, the rain-stone
19. Stone platform with three old cannons
20. Bangka dari, place of the original settlement
     and the resting-spot for the earth-spirits
21. Large trees
22. Toto-stone
23. Graveyard of Todo
24. House for the gong

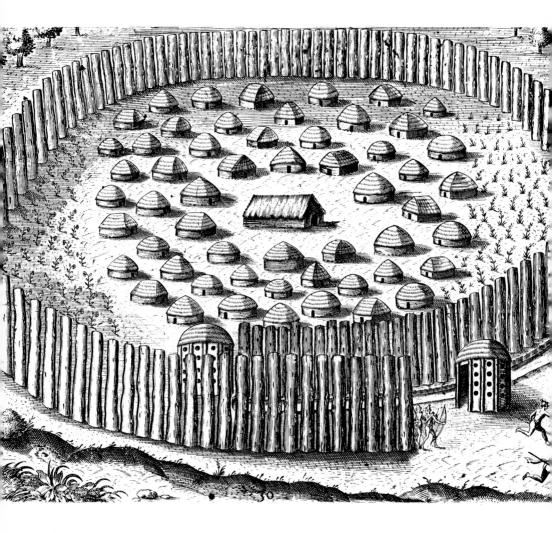

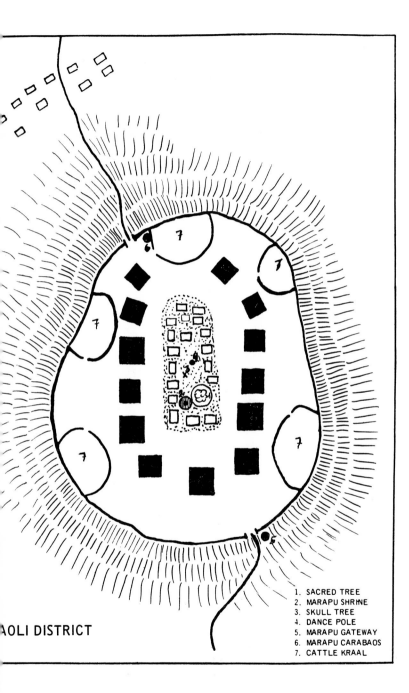

AOLI DISTRICT

1. SACRED TREE
2. MARAPU SHRINE
3. SKULL TREE
4. DANCE POLE
5. MARAPU GATEWAY
6. MARAPU CARABAOS
7. CATTLE KRAAL

78. View of Onondaga fortified village. Iroquois Confederacy, New York State.

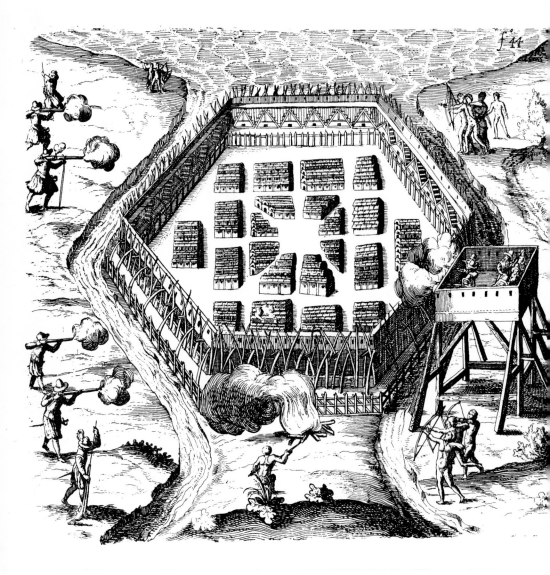

MALI

DOGON

GUINEA   SENUFO   GHANA   NIGERIA   MATAKAM   SUDAN
         KONIAGI   YORUBA   BENIN   MOUSGOUM   NUBA
GBANDE   MASSA
LIBERIA   CAMEROUN
                              BAMILEKE

                                   MBUTI

                         CONGO
                                LEGA
                                        TANZANIA

                                   ZAMBIA
                                ILA

                         RHODESIA

         AMBO
    HERERO
         HEIKUM !KUNG BUSHMEN

    SOUTH WEST
    AFRICA   SWAZI
                      ZULU

         SOUTH AFRICA

AFRICA

Map A

CHINA

TONKIN

MICRONESIA

NIAS

BATAK

BORNEO

CELEBES

INDONESIA

BALI   FLORES

SUMBA

NEW GUINEA

GURURUMA

RORO MAILU

NEW BRITAIN

TROBRIAND
IS.

MELANES

AUSTRALIA

NEW CALE

NEW

Map B

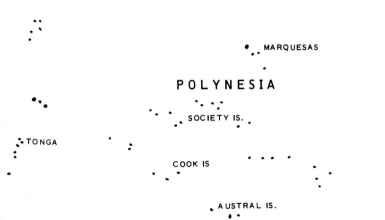

HAWAII

MARQUESAS

POLYNESIA

SOCIETY IS.

TONGA

COOK IS

AUSTRAL IS.

EASTER I.

TLINGIT

NORTHWEST COAST

HAIDA

KWAKIUTL

SALISH

CHEYENNE

PLAINS

OMAHA

OSAGE

ONONDAGA

CLIFF DWELLERS

PUEBLO

POMEIOCK

TIMUQUANAN

MESOAMERICA

AMAZON BASIN

KARAJA

SHAVANTE

BORORO

THE NEW WORLD

Map C

NOTES

1. "Primitive world" is used here merely as a conventional designation for the traditional societies of Africa, Southeast Asia, Oceania, and the New World that, until recently, had not been strongly influenced by the high cultures of Europe, Asia, or pre-Columbian America. The use of the term "primitive" does not denote any qualitative judgment whatsoever about these societies or their individual members.

2. Robin Horton, "African Traditional Thought and Western Science," *Africa* 37, Nos. 1 and 2, 1967, pp. 50–71; 155–187, and R. H. Stone, *Yoruba Lore and the Universe*, Occasional Paper No. 4, University of Ibadan Institute of Education, 1965, pp. 8–9, have called attention to this pattern of thinking. At the same time, we should not regard these societies as totally fatalistic; primitive man often believed he could change or affect the world.

3. For further details, see the discussion of Mailu, New Guinea, pp. 27–29.

4. E. P. Chinnery, *Anthropological Report No. 1*, Territory of New Guinea, Melbourne, 1927.

5. Philip L. Newman, *Knowing the Gururumba*, New York, 1960, pp. 18–20; H. Labouret, "Afrique occidentale et équatorial" in *L'habitation indigène dans les possessions françaises*, 1931, p. 38; and Alice G. James, *Village Arrangement and Social Organization Among Some Amazon Tribes*, New York, 1947, pp. 58–60.

6. For further remarks on this method, see Claude Lévi-Strauss, *Structural Anthropology*, New York, 1963, reprinted 1967, especially Chapters 1, 3, 8, and 15.

7. This account of the Mbuti Pygmies relies almost entirely on Colin Turnbull, *The Forest People*, London, 1961; *Wayward Servants*, Philadelphia, 1965; and *The Mbuti Pygmies: An Ethnographic Survey*, Anthropological Papers of the American Museum of Natural History, Vol. 50, Part 3, 1965, pp. 137–282.

8. V. Gordon Childe, *Man Makes Himself*, London, 1936, reprinted New York, 1951, pp. 45–86, and other works. It should be noted, however, that Turnbull cautions against interpreting Mbuti social structure as a Stone Age survival, because of their long interaction with adjacent agricultural groups.

9. Turnbull, *Wayward Servants*, p. 85 and Fig. 8.

10. Paul Schebesta, *Die Bambuti Pygmäen vom Ituri: Die Wirtschaft der Ituri Bambuti*, Memoires Inst. Royal Col. Belge, Sec. Sci., Morales et Politiques, Ser. 4, Vol. 2; Ser. 1, Vol. 2, Part 1, pp. 1–284, especially pp. 132–133, notes that other Pygmy groups build their huts in a distinctly circular pattern.

11. For a detailed discussion, see Turnbull, *Wayward Servants*, pp. 100–107 and plans.

12. Turnbull, *Wayward Servants*, p. 200, footnote 6.

13. It would be dangerous, however, not to recognize that Bushman culture has been considerably modified over the centuries due to contact with other peoples. There are, of course, many differences between the forest-dwelling Pygmy and the *veldt*-inhabiting Bushman, not the least significant being the complete absence of visual art among the Mbuti, whereas the Bushman created the impressive rock paintings and petroglyphs of southern Africa. On the other hand, the musical forms of the two groups show certain similarities, notably the use of yodelling.

14. This discussion is largely based on Lorna Marshall, "!Kung Bushman Bands," *Africa*, Vol. 30, Oct. 1960, pp. 325–355.

15. Marshall, "!Kung Bushman Bands," pp. 342–344. There is a tendency, however, for !Kung *scherms* to face the center of the *werf*.

16. I am indebted to Nicholas England for this and many other observations on Bushman culture. For further details, see his *Music Among the Zhu'/' wa-si of South West Africa and Botswana*, unpublished doctoral dissertation, Harvard University, 1968.

17. G. W. Stow, *The Native Races of South Africa*, London, 1905, and D. F. Ellenberger, *History of the Basuto*, 1912, cited in J. Walton, *African Village*, Pretoria, 1956, pp. 12–14.

18. E. Adamson Hoebel, *The Cheyennes: Indians of the Great Plains*, New York, 1960, pp. 1–3. Our description refers to conditions that prevailed about one hundred years ago.

19. George Dorsey, "The Cheyenne," *Field Columbian Museum, Anthropological Series*, Vol. 9, No. 2, 1905, pp. 186–187.

20. Of all Plains groups, only the Comanche did not employ the camp circle, according to G. B. Grinnell, *The Cheyenne Indians*, New Haven, 1923, Vol. 2, p. 90. Grinnell adds that the opening in the Cheyenne circle faced east or southeast.

21. George Dorsey, "The Cheyenne," Vol. 9, No. 2, 1905, pp. 61–62.

22. R. and G. Laubin, *The Indian Tipi*, Norman, Oklahoma, 1957, p. 183.

23. Hoebel and Grinnell state that there were ten divisions, but they disagree as to details. George Dorsey, "The Cheyenne," 1905, and James Mooney, "The Cheyenne Indians," *American Anthropological Association Memoirs*, Vol. 1, Part 6, 1907, offer the figures of thirteen and eleven respectively. R. Lowie, *Indians of the Plains*, New York, 1963, pp. 93–94, claims there were eleven divisions, but his diagram taken from Dorsey illustrates only five. Cheyenne informants themselves disagree as to the number, according to Hoebel.

24. See J. O. Dorsey, "Camp Circles of Siouan Tribes," *American Anthropologist*, old series 2, 1889, p. 175, and "Omaha Sociology," *Bureau of American Ethnology Third Annual Report*, 1881–1882. See also Alice Fletcher and Francis La Flesche, "The Omaha Tribe," *Bureau of American Ethnology 27th Annual Report*, 1905–1906.

25. James Mooney, "Calendar History of the Kiowa Indians," *Bureau of American Ethnology 17th Annual Report*, 1895–1896, pp. 228–229.

26. James A. Teit, "The Salishan Tribes of the Western Plateau," *Bureau of American Ethnology 49th Annual Report*, 1927–28, p. 155.

27. Aurel Krause, *Die Tlinkit Indianer*, Jena, 1885, trans. by E. Gunther, 1956, p. 86, notes that "some consist of only a few houses which are set in a single row, others have as many as 50 to 60 houses of varying sizes which are arranged in two more or less regular rows, for the houses of each clan form a separate group." George Emmons, "The Whale House of the Chilkat," *Anthropological Papers of the American Museum of Natural History*, Vol. 19, 1, 1916, p. 18, states that the houses follow the shore. A sketch of Sitka, dated 1869 and published in the "Alaskan Coast Pilot" (American Museum of Natural History Neg. No. 124885) shows the houses disposed in a random manner but facing the beach.

28. Joan Vastokas, *Architecture of the Northwest Coast Indians of America*, unpublished doctoral dissertation, Columbia University, 1966, p. 18, to which I am indebted for many references. The Quinalt, situated at approximately the southern edge of the Northwest Coast, scattered their houses in an irregular row ten to twenty yards from the bank (R. Olsen, "The Quinalt Indians," *University of Washington Publications in Anthropology*, Vol. 6, No. 1, 1936, p. 95); the long axis of these houses, however, was always aligned from east to west.

29. Most of the information given here is taken from Wilson Duff and Michael Kew, *Anthony Island, A Home of the Haidas*, reprinted from *Report of the Provincial Museum of Natural History and Anthropology for 1957*, Victoria, 1958, pp. 1–28; and John Swanton, *Ethnology of the Haida*, Jessup North Pacific Expedition, Vol. 5, Part 1, 1905.

30. According to Swanton, *Ethnology of the Haida*, 1905, p. 68, Haida chiefs' houses were generally in the center of the row, but G. Dawson, *Report on the Queen Charlotte Islands 1878, Geological Survey of Canada*, 1880, p. 116, denies that this was the case. Vastokas, *Architecture of the Northwest Coast Indians of America*, p. 32, points out that the second Haida house-type was also used by the Kaigani Haida, who apparently migrated to Prince of Wales Island several hundred years ago and thus may be an older type. But since this

type of dwelling was also used by the Tlingit (Vastokas, *Architecture of the Northwest Coast Indians of America*, p. 34) its presence on Anthony Island may be due to a more recent infiltration of Tlingit influences.

31. Population density figures are difficult to verify: in 1787, George Dixon counted 180 people in eleven canoes. Three hundred men are supposed to have participated in an attack on the "Union" and at least one hundred died in battles between 1791 and 1795. The disastrous smallpox epidemics of the 1860's reduced Haida populations by at least two thirds. By 1884 there were only thirty inhabitants and the site was soon abandoned. The figures quoted assume that all of the houses were domiciles and not mortuary houses. All of these data are subject to question but are cited in the absence of anything better.

32. For parallel aesthetics in other visual arts, see Paul S. Wingert, "Tsimshian Sculptures," in *The Tsimshian: Their Arts and Music*, The American Ethnological Society, Vol. 18, New York, 1951, reprinted in *The Tsimshian and their Art*, University of Washington, Seattle, 1966. Since visitors would have seen the Haida village first from its seaward aspect, it may be assumed that this was the primary planning vista. Vastokas, *Architecture of the Northwest Coast Indians of America*, pp. 92–93, 99–102, stresses the rigidity of the Haida social organization and village plan, whereas I tend to see it as a reconciliation of disparate forces. My discussion is nevertheless indebted to hers in many respects.

33. Cf. the works of Leonhard Adam, Miguel Covarrubias, Carl Hentze, Robert Heine-Geldern, Carl Schuster, Douglas Fraser, Mino Badner, and the forthcoming *Early Chinese Art and Its Possible Influence in the Pacific Basin*, Proceedings of an International Symposium held at Columbia University in August, 1967.

34. W. J. V. Saville, *In Unknown New Guinea*, Philadelphia, 1926, pp. 23–45 ff., is the principal source on the Mailu village. This discussion refers to conditions in Saville's time and employs the kinship terminology used by him.

35. See Murray Groves, "Motuan Pottery," *Journal of the Polynesian Society*, Vol. 69, 1960, pp. 2–22, for a recent discussion.

36. B. Malinowski, "The Natives of Mailu: Preliminary Results of the Robert Mond Research Work in British New Guinea," *Transactions and Proceedings of the Royal Society of South Australia*, Vol. 39, 1915, pp. 494–706; and Raymond Firth, "Notes on the Social Structure of Some South-Eastern New Guinea Communities," *Man*, Vol. 52, 1952, pp. 65–67, 86–89.

37. C. G. Seligman, *The Melanesians of British New Guinea*, Cambridge, 1910, p. 198. For some Pacific plans, see Anneliese Eilers, *Inseln um Ponape: Ergebnisse der Südsee Expedition 1908–10*, Hamburg, 1934. Other examples are discussed in C. Schmitz, "Balam: Der Tanz- und Kultplatz in Melanesien als Versammlungsort und mimischer Schauplatz," *Die Schaubühne*, Vol. 46, 1955, pp. 31–35; and A. Bühler, "Der Platz als bestimmender Faktor von Siedlungsformen in Ostindonesien und Melanesien," *Regio Basiliensis* 1/2, 1960, pp. 202–212. Polynesia suffered acculturation at such an early date that not much is known about traditional village plans there except as described in Irmgard Moschner, *Haus und Siedlung in Polynesien*, typescript, Inst. für Völkerkunde, Vienna, 1949. Eric K. Reed, "Types of Village-Plan Layouts in the Southwest," in G. Willey (ed.) *Prehistoric Settlement Plans in the New World*, 1956, pp. 11–17, notes that parallel alignments are characteristic of Micronesian villages.

38. Authorities disagree greatly as to the dates of the Austronesian dispersal. The figures are cited merely to indicate the general time span involved.

39. C. G. Seligman, *The Melanesians of British New Guinea*, p. 696.

40. B. Malinowski, *The Sexual Life of Savages in Northwestern Melanesia*, London, 1929, reprinted New York, n.d., pp. 8–22; and *Coral Gardens and their Magic*, Vol. I, London, 1935, Fig. 12.

41. Paul S. Wingert has pointed out that a similar preference for curvilinear movement appears in Trobriand dance patterns. Malinowski paid relatively little attention to material culture and art, preferring to stress function and

social relations. For a somewhat similar plan in the southern Massim area, see R. F. Fortune, *Sorcerers of Dobu*, London, 1932, reprinted New York, 1963, Fig. 1.

42. Malinowski, *The Sexual Life of Savages*, pp. 130–133. C. Lévi-Strauss, *Structural Anthropology*, 1963, chapter 8, criticizes Malinowski's view, but himself overlooks the historical explanation given here.

43. H. R. van Heekeren, *The Bronze Iron Age of Indonesia*, Verhandelingen van het Koninklijk Instituut voor Taal-, Land- en Volkenkunde 22, 1958, pp. 16–34; John Haskins, "Cache at Stone-fortress-hill," *Natural History*, Feb. 1963, pp. 30–39; R. Heine-Geldern, "Archaeology and Art of Sumatra," *Wiener Beiträge zur Kulturgeschichte und Linguistik*, III, pp. 316–322.

44. V. Goloubew, "L'âge du bronze au Tonkin et dans le Nord-Annam," *Bullétin de l'École Française d'Extrême Orient* 29, pp. 1–46; R. Heine-Geldern, "L'art prébouddhique de la Chine et de l'Asie du Sud-Est et son influence en Océanie," *Revue des Arts Asiatiques* 11, 1937, pp. 177–206; "Indonesian Culture," *Encyclopedia of World Art*, Vol. 8, cols. 41–59; and "Some Tribal Art Styles of Southeast Asia," in D. Fraser (ed.), *The Many Faces of Primitive Art: A Critical Anthology*, Englewood Cliffs, 1966, pp. 165–221.

45. See Douglas Fraser, *Primitive Art*, 1962, pp. 193–194, and "The Heraldic Woman: A Study in Diffusion," in *The Many Faces of Primitive Art: A Critical Anthology*, p. 70. I am indebted to Sarah Gill of the University of Hawaii for developing many of these ideas in an unpublished term paper, "Bwayma, The Trobriand Yam House," Columbia University, 1963. Saddle-roofed houses are found in several other parts of New Guinea (Aitape, Middle Sepik, Central District) but these, too, are clearly intrusive.

46. For ethnographic details, see E. M. Loeb, "Sumatra: Its History and People," *Wiener Beiträge zur Kulturgeschichte und Linguistik*, III, 1935, pp. 128–158.

47. P. Suzuki, *The Religious System and Culture of Nias, Indonesia*, Ph. D. thesis, Leiden University, The Hague, 1959, p. 56 ff., on which this account of Nias planning is heavily dependent.

48. E. E. W. Gs. Schroder, *Nias, Ethnographische, Geographische en Historische Aanteekeningen en Studien*, I, Leiden, 1917, p. 95.

49. F. M. Schnitger, *Forgotten Kingdoms in Sumatra*, 1939, reprinted Leiden, 1964, p. 155.

50. Thomas Thomsen, "Hili Mondregeraja og dens Høvdinghus," *Report*, National-al Museet, Copenhagen, 1928, No. 2, pp. 51–62, esp. p. 55. Thomsen was told by Møller that the forecourt was a recent innovation of the present chief, who shifted his house to the center of the village. Noblemen who could not find room at this end of the village were nevertheless accommodated on the right-hand or upper-world side.

51. Hans Schärer, *Ngaju Religion: The Conception of God Among a South Borneo People*, trans. Rodney Needham, The Hague, 1963, pp. 64–66.

52. Roger Yong Djiet Tan, "Description and Comparative Analysis of the Domestic Architecture of South Bali," M. A. thesis, Yale University, 1966, portions of which have been published in the *Bijdragen tot de Taal-, Land- en Volkenkunde*, The Hague, Vol. 123, 1967, pp. 442–475.

53. The method used by Tan of extrapolating essential features from the material has been employed extensively by Dutch scholars of religion and history for several decades. C. Geetz, "Form and Variation in Balinese Village Structure," *American Anthropologist* 61, 1959, pp. 991–1012, footnotes 12 and 13, criticizes this method as failing to recognize the importance of local adaptation. However, Geetz's own argument suggests that the similarities of planning in such diverse areas as Nias, Borneo, Sumatra, and Bali cannot possibly be due to adaptation and must therefore reflect an older common heritage.

54. As Tan points out, a twofold division of structures into houses and granaries is characteristic of other Indonesian peoples such as the Toradja of Celebes and the Batak of Sumatra. See Figs. 37–39 and D. W. N. de Boer, "Het Toba-Bataksche Huis," *Encyclopaedisch Bureau*, Mededeelingen, Afl. 23, 1920, Pl. 35.

55. Robert Heine-Geldern, *Conceptions of State and Kingship in Southeast Asia*, Data Paper No. 18, Cornell University Southeast Asia Program, 1956, pp. 1–14, argues that this concept originated in the ancient Near East, perhaps in the fourth millennium B. C., and subsequently affected the cosmological planning of India, China, Southeast Asia, and Europe. Similar ideas, it should be noted, appear in the cosmology and urban planning of pre-Columbian Mesoamerica (cf. Heine-Geldern, "Weltbild und Bauform in Südostasien," *Wiener Beiträge zur Kunst- und Kulturgeschichte Asiens* IV, 1930, pp. 28–78, and Walter Krickeberg, "Bauform und Weltbild im alten Mexico," *Paideuma* 4, 1950, pp. 295–333.)

56. For east and south Africa, see James Walton, *African Village*, Pretoria, 1956, and R. U. Light, *Focus on Africa*, New York, 1944; for west Africa, Herta Haselberger, *Bautraditionen der westafrikanischen Negerkulturen*, Wissenschaftliche Schriftenreihe des Afro-Asiatischen Institut, Vienna, 1964.

57. H. Haselberger, *Bautraditionen*, p. 98.

58. T. J. Bowen, *Central Africa, Adventures and Missionary Labours in Several Countries in the Interior of Africa from 1849 to 1856*, Charleston, 1857, p. 218; and A. L. Mabogunje, *Yoruba Towns*, Ibadan University, 1962, p. 8.

59. For a review of the criteria used by various scholars, see Jorge Hardoy, *Ciudades Precolumbinas*, Buenos Aires, 1964, pp. 15–23, and Gideon Sjoberg, *The Pre-Industrial City*, Glencoe, Illinois, 1960, pp. 13–18.

60. W. J. Sanders, "The Central Mexican Symbiotic Region: A Study in Prehistoric Settlement Patterns," in G. Willey (ed.), *Prehistoric Settlement Patterns in the New World*, Viking Fund Publication 23, 1956, pp. 114–127, suggests the figure of seventy-five percent non-farmers having heterogeneous occupations.

61. This description refers primarily to the Yoruba of Oyo, the major kingdom in the north.

62. William Bascom, "Urbanism as a Traditional African Pattern," *Sociological Review*, Vol. 7, No. 1, July, 1959, p. 41.

63. Samuel Johnson, *The History of the Yorubas*, written ca. 1891 by a Yoruba, published Lagos, 1921, p. 22. Johnson, p. 93, adds that the towns of eastern Yorubaland (the Ile-Ife, Ilesha, and Ekiti kingdoms) preserved their town plans far better than the western kingdoms of the Oyo and Egba Yoruba which suffered numerous wars in the nineteenth century.

64. Mabogunje, *Yoruba Towns*, p. 5 and footnote. See also G. J. A. Ojo, *Yoruba Culture: A Geographical Analysis*, London, 1966, esp. chapter 6, "The Layout and Morphology of Yoruba Towns," pp. 131–157.

65. Hugh Clapperton, *Journal of a Second Expedition into the Interior of Africa*, London, 1829, p. 58, observed that the palace grounds at Old Oyo were "about a mile square ... having two large parks, one in front and another facing the north." For a discussion of the relation of the Yoruba palace grounds to the town, see G. J. A. Ojo, *Yoruba Palaces*, London, 1966, pp. 22–55.

66. T. J. Bowen, *Central Africa, Adventures and Missionary Labours...*, p. 146. The information on Ketu is summarized in M. Palau-Marti, *Le roi-dieu au Bénin*, Paris, 1962, pp. 41–47.

67. Palau-Marti, *Le roi-dieu au Bénin*, pp. 52–54, 177–178.

68. On the possible migration of these ideas and forms, see P. Mercier, "The Fon of Dahomey," in D. Forde (ed.), *African Worlds*, London, 1954, reprinted 1965, p. 215; Douglas Fraser, *Primitive Art*, pp. 99–103; *The Many Faces of Primitive Art: A Critical Anthology*, pp. 46–47; and "The Fishlegged Figure in Benin and Yoruba Art" in D. Fraser and H. M. Cole (eds.), *Art and Leadership in Africa*, (forthcoming). Although there is always the possibility of convergence with or contamination by European myths, the story of the creation of man from clay and the dispatching of birds to investigate the footing, described by Phillips Stevens, "Orisha-Nla Festival," *Nigeria Magazine* No. 90, Sept. 1966, pp. 184–185, are remarkably reminiscent of biblical accounts and their Near-Eastern prototypes. S. O. Biobaku, using the extensive Yoruba myths concerning the Kisra migration, concludes that the Yoruba moved from the Near East

between A. D. 600–1000, but probably only a small elite group actually made the journey.

69. H. Vedder, "The Herero," *The Native Tribes of South-West Africa*, Capetown, 1928, pp. 153–211. The same direction is favored by the Swazi of South Africa; see Hilda Kuper, "The Architecture of Swaziland," *Architectural Review*, Vol. 100, July, 1946, pp. 20–24.

70. B. A. G. Vroklage, "De Prauw in de Culturen van Flores," *Cultureel Indië*, Vol. 2, 1940, pp. 193–199; 230–234; 263–270. A similar ship concept probably underlies the plan of Todo village in west Flores, which we illustrate in Fig. 74; see W. van Bekkum, *Manggaraische Kunst*, Indisch Instituut Med. 68, Afd. Volkenk. No. 21, Leiden, 1946, pp. 1–8.

71. E. B. O'Callaghan, *The Documentary History of New York*, Albany, 1850, Vol. 3, p. 14. The engraving from Samuel Champlain's volume obviously distorts the Indian village plan in the direction of a European radially-planned polygonal fortress.

RECOMMENDED READING

The literature on village planning in the primitive world is extremely particularistic and is scattered through countless books and articles. The following is only intended, therefore, to give a basic orientation in the field. For information on planning in specific societies, the reader must consult the anthropological, geographical, and art-historical bibliographies available for each area.

AFRICA

Beguin, J. *et al*, *L'habitat au Cameroun*. Paris, 1951.
Frobenius, Leo, *Das unbekannte Afrika*. Munich, 1923.
Haselberger, Herta, *Bautraditionen der westafrikanischen Negerkulturen*. Afro-Asiatisches Institut. Vienna, 1964.
Labouret, H., "Afrique occidentale et équatoriale," in *L'habitation indigène dans les possessions françaises*. Paris, 1931, pp. 21–43.
Light, Richard U., *Focus on Africa*. American Geographical Society, New York, 2nd edition, 1944.
Schachtzabel, Alfred, *Die Siedlungsverhältnisse der Bantu-Neger*. Supplement to *Internationales Archiv für Ethnographie*, Vol. 20, Leiden, 1911.
Walton, James, *African Village*. Pretoria, 1956.

SOUTHEAST ASIA—OCEANIA

Behrmann, Walter, "Die Wohnstätten der Eingeborenen im Innern von Neu-Guinea," [Sepik] *Festband Albrecht Penck*, Stuttgart, 1918, pp. 324–339.
Bühler, Alfred, "Der Platz als bestimmender Faktor von Siedlungsformen in Ostindonesien und Melanesien," *Regio Basiliensis*, 1/2, 1960, pp. 202–212.

118

Leenhardt, Maurice, "L'habitation indigène en Océanie," in *L'habitation indigène dans les possessions françaises*, Paris, 1931, pp. 91–111.

Moschner, Irmgard, *Haus und Siedlung in Polynesien*. Unpublished typescript. Institut für Völkerkunde. Vienna, 1949.

Naval Intelligence Division, *Pacific Islands*. 4 vols. London, 1943–45.

Schmitz, Carl, "Balam. Der Tanz- und Kultplatz in Melanesien als Versammlungsort und mimischer Schauplatz," *Die Schaubühne*, Vol. 46, 1955.

Tillema, H. F., *Kromoblanda, Over 't vraagstuk van "het Wonen" in Kromo's groote land*. 5 vols. in 6 parts. The Hague, 1915–1922.

NEW WORLD

James, Alice G., *Village Arrangement and Social Organization Among Some Amazon Tribes*. New York, 1949.

Lévi-Strauss, Claude, "Do Dual Organizations Exist?" *Structural Anthropology*. New York, 1963, Chapter 8.

Morgan, Lewis, *Houses and House-Life of the American Aborgines*. Contributions to North American Ethnology. Washington, 1881. Reprinted Chicago, 1965.

Reed, Erik K., "Types of Village-Plan Layouts in the Southwest," in *Prehistoric Settlement Patterns in the New World*, ed. G. Willey. Chicago, 1956, pp. 11–17.

Sarfert, Ernst, "Haus und Dorf bei den Eingeborenen Nordamerikas," *Archiv für Anthropologie*, n.f., Vol. 7, pts. 2 & 3, 1908, pp. 119–215.

Stubbs, Stanley A., *Bird's-Eye View of the Pueblos*. Norman, Oklahoma, 1950.

LIST OF ILLUSTRATIONS

ing after Backhouse by James Walton, *African Village*, J. L. van Schaik, Pretoria, 1956, Fig. 5.

16. Plan of Bushman *werf*. Kalahari desert, Africa. From: Nicholas England, *Music Among the Zhu'/' wa-si of South West Africa and Botswana*, unpublished doctoral dissertation, Harvard University, 1968, Chapter V, Fig. 37. Drawn by Roger Y. D. Tan.

17. Cheyenne camp. Western Plains, United States. Photograph by William S. Soulé, c. 1867–74, Smithsonian Institution, Bureau of American Ethnology, Washington, D. C.

18. Plan of Cheyenne camp circle. Western Plains, United States. From: George A. Dorsey, "The Cheyenne," *Field Columbian Museum, Anthropological Series*, Vol. 9, No. 2, Chicago, 1905, Pl. XIX.

19. Plan showing four different arrangements of camp circles. Plains Indians. From: Reginald and Gladys Laubin, *The Indian Tipi: Its History, Construction, and Use*, Copyright 1957 by the University of Oklahoma Press, Norman, Oklahoma, Fig. 45.

20. Plan of ancient Cheyenne camp circle. Western Plains, United States. From: George A. Dorsey "The Cheyenne," *Field Columbian Museum, Anthropological Series*, Vol. 9, No. 1, Chicago, 1905, Pl. XVII.

21. Plan of Cheyenne camp circle. Western Plains, United States. From: George B. Grinnell, *The Cheyenne Indians*, Yale University Press, New Haven, 1923, p. 90.

22. Plan of Cheyenne camp circle during election of chiefs. Western Plains, United States. From: George A. Dorsey, "The Cheyenne," *Field Columbian Museum, Anthropological Series*, Vol. 9, No. 1, Chicago, 1905, Pl. II.

23. Village sites on Anthony Island. Haida, Queen Charlotte Islands, British Columbia, Canada. From: Wilson Duff and Michael Kew, *Anthony Island, A Home of the Haidas*, reprinted from *Report of the Provincial Museum of Natural History for 1957*, Victoria, 1958, Map 2.

24. Second village at Skidegate. Haida, Queen Charlotte Islands, British Columbia, Canada. Photo: Provincial Archives, Victoria, B.C.

25. Plan of Ninstints village. Haida, Queen Charlotte Islands, British Columbia, Canada. From: Wilson Duff and Michael Kew, *Anthony Island, A Home of the Haidas*, reprinted from *Report of the Provincial Museum of Natural History for 1957*, Victoria, 1958, Map 3.

26. Mailu Island Village. Papua, New Guinea. Photo: American Museum of Natural History, New York..

27. Mailu Island Village. Papua, New Guinea. Photo: American Museum of Natural History, New York.

28. Plan showing the disposition of the four village clans and their subdivisions. Mailu Island Village, Papua, New Guinea. From: W. J. V. Saville, *In Unknown New Guinea*, J. P. Lippincott Company, Philadelphia, 1926, p. 31.

29. Mailu Island Village street. Papua, New Guinea. Photo: American Museum of Natural History, New York.

30. Street with clubhouse. Möu village, Roro, Papua, New Guinea. Photo: Field Museum of Natural History, Chicago.

31. Plan of Boru village. Baxter Bay, Papua, New Guinea. After Raymond Firth, "Notes on the Social Structure of Some South-Eastern New Guinea

Communities," *Man*, 52, May, 1952, Art. 99, Fig. 1. Redrawn by Roger Y. D. Tan.

32. Barakau village, about twenty miles east of Port Moresby. Papua, New Guinea. Photo: American Museum of Natural History, New York.

33. Village in mangrove swamp. Marshalls Lagoon, Papua, New Guinea. Photo: Field Museum of Natural History, Chicago.

34. Plan of Omarakana village. Kiriwina district, Trobriand Islands, New Guinea. From: B. Malinowski, *The Sexual Life of Savages in Northwest Melanesia*, Harcourt, Brace & World, Inc., New York, n.d. Fig. 1.

35. Yam houses. Kiriwina district, Trobriand Islands, New Guinea. From: C. G. Seligman, *The Melanesians of British New Guinea*, Cambridge University Press, Cambridge, 1910, Pl. LXXVI.

36. Karo Batak village. Sumatra, Indonesia. From: H. F. Tillema, *Kromoblanda*, Vol. 5, pt. 2, The Hague, 1922, p. 562.

37. Plan of a Karo Batak village. Sumatra, Indonesia. All houses are parallel to a nearby river. Drawn by Roger Y. D. Tan from data supplied by V. R. van Romondt.

38. Sa'dan Toradja village. Central Celebes, Indonesia. Photo: Tropenmuseum, Amsterdam.

39. Plan of a Sa'dan Toradja village. Drawn by Roger Y. D. Tan from data supplied by V. R. van Romondt.

40. Village of Hili Mondregeraja, south Nias, Indonesia. Photo: National Museum, Copenhagen.

41. Plan of Bawamataluö village in South Nias. Drawn by Roger Y. D. Tan from data supplied by V. R. van Romondt.

42. Village of Hili Mondregeraja. South Nias, Indonesia. Photo: National Museum, Copenhagen.

43. Schematic plan of Bali Aga village. Bali, Indonesia. Drawn by Roger Y. D. Tan.

44. Plan of Tenganan village. Bali, Indonesia. Drawn by Roger Y. D. Tan.

45. Plan of Toba Batak village on Samosir Island. Sumatra, Indonesia. Drawn by Roger Y. D. Tan from data supplied by V. R. van Romondt.

46. Plan of chief's village, "At the Place of Rumours." Swaziland, South Africa. From: Hilda Kuper, "The Architecture of Swaziland," *Architectural Review*, Vol. 100, July, 1946, p. 24.

47. Swazi *kraals*. Near Bremersdorp, South Africa. Photo: Richard U. Light, American Geographical Society, New York.

48. Zulu *kraal*. South Africa. Photo: Richard U. Light, American Geographical Society, New York.

49. Ambo *kraals*. South West Africa. From a drawing by James Walton, *African Village*, J. L. van Schaik, Pretoria, 1956, Fig. 57.

50. Pit circles. Rhodesia. From a drawing by James Walton, *African Village*, J. L. van Schaik, Pretoria, 1956, Fig. 42.

51. Nuba ring homesteads. Kordofan, Sudan, Africa. From a drawing after Nadel by James Walton, *African Village*, J. L. van Schaik, Pretoria, 1956, Fig. 44.

52. Plan of Massa homestead. Yagoua, Cameroun, Africa. From: J. Beguin, *et al. L'habitat au Cameroun*, Office de la Recherche Scientifique et Technique Outre-Mer, Paris, 1951, p. 43.

53. Plan of Mousgoum homestead. Gaïa, Cameroun, Africa. From: J. Beguin, *et al. L'habitat au Cameroun*, Office de la Recherche Scientifique et Technique Outre-Mer, Paris, 1951, p. 34.

54. Plan of Matakam homestead. Cameroun, Africa. From: J. Beguin, *et al. L'habitat au Cameroun*, Office de la Recherche Scientifique et Technique Outre-Mer, Paris, 1951, p. 23.

55. Plan of Gbande (Bande) fortified town Sambatahun. Northern Liberia, Africa. From: H. Haselberger, *Bautraditionen der westafrikanischen Negerkulturen*, Afro-Asiatisches Inst., Vienna, 1964, Fig. 55.

56. Plan of Senufo village near Sikasso. Mali, Africa. From: H. Haselberger, *Bautraditionen der westafrikanischen Negerkulturen*, Afro-Asiatisches Inst., Vienna, 1964, Fig. 56 (copyright Frobenius-Institut, Frankfurt/M).

57. Plan of Ashanti hamlet. Ghana, Africa. From: H. Haselberger, *Bautraditionen der westafrikanischen Negerkulturen*, Afro-Asiatisches Inst., Vienna, 1964, Fig. 41 (copyright Frobenius-Institut, Frankfurt/M).

58. Benin City. Nigeria, Africa. From: J. Ogilby, *Africa*, London, 1670, following p. 470.

59. Plan of Benin City and the royal palace. Nigeria, Africa. From a plan after Dennett in M. Palau Marti, *Le roi-dieu au Bénin*, Editions Berger-Levrault, Paris, 1964, p. 69.

60. Aerial view of Benin City. Nigeria, Africa. Photo: Federal Ministry of Works and Housing, Lagos.

61. Aerial view of Mukobela's village. Ila, Zambia, Africa. Photo: Richard U. Light, American Geographical Society, New York.

62. Aerial view of Mukobela's village. Ila, Zambia, Africa. Photo: Mary Light, American Geographical Society, New York.

63. Plan of Ilesha showing relation of palace (Afin) to chief's compounds. Yoruba, Nigeria, Africa. From: G. J. A. Ojo, *Yoruba Palaces*, University of London Press, London, 1966, Fig. 4.

64. Aerial view of Ilesha. Yoruba, Nigeria, Africa. Photo: Federal Ministry of Works and Housing, Lagos.

65. Aerial view of Oyo. Yoruba, Nigeria, Africa. Photo: Federal Ministry of Works and Housing, Lagos.

66. Plan of compounds around Afin Oyo (Oyo palace). Yoruba, Nigeria, Africa. From: G. J. A. Ojo, *Yoruba Palaces*, University of London Press, London, 1966, Fig. 12.

67. Plan of Owo. Yoruba, Nigeria, Africa. From G. J. A. Ojo, *Yoruba Palaces*, University of London Press, London, 1966, Fig. 5.

68. Plan of Ile-Ife. Yoruba, Nigeria, Africa. From: Frank Willett, *Ife in the History of West African Sculpture*, Thames and Hudson, London, 1967, p. 16.

69. Plan of Ado-Ekiti. Yoruba, Nigeria, Africa. From: G. J. A. Ojo, *Yoruba Palaces*, University of London Press, London, 1966, Fig. 3.

70. Schematic plan of Ketu. Yoruba, Dahomey, Africa. From: M. Palau Marti, *Le roi-dieu au Bénin*, Editions Berger-Levrault, Paris, 1964, p. 45.

71. Watercolor of Pomeiock town by John White, c. 1585. North Carolina. Photo: The British Museum, London.

72. Plan of Bororo village. South central Brazil. From: Claude Lévi-Strauss, *Structural Anthropology*, Basic Books, Inc., New York, 1963, Fig. 9.

73. Aerial view of Shavante village. Matto Grosso, central Brazil. Photo: American Museum of Natural History, New York.

74. Plan of Todo village. Manggarai, Flores, Indonesia. From: W. van Bekkum, *Manggaraische Kunst*, E. J. Brill, Leiden, 1946, Sketch 1 (copyright Tropenmuseum, Amsterdam).

75. Drawing of Maori fortified village. New Zealand. From a drawing by S. Parkinson, c. 1769, British Museum Add. ms. 23920. Courtesy of the Trustees of the British Museum.

76. View of fortified village. Timuquanan Indians, Florida. Engraving by Theodore De Bry, c. 1590, from a painting by J. Le Moyne. Photo: American Museum of Natural History, New York.

77. Ideal plan of a traditional ancestral village (*praing* = progenitors' village). Laoli district, West Sumba, Indonesia. Unpublished drawing courtesy Alfred Bühler.

78. View of Onondaga fortified village. Iroquois Confederacy, New York State. From: Samuel de Champlain, *Voyages et descouvertures faites en la Nouvelle France*, Paris, 1627, preceding fol. 44.

Map A. Africa.
Map B. Southeast Asia-Oceania.
Map C. The New World.
Drawn by Roger Y. D. Tan.

INDEX

This index is not designed to be easy to use. Indexing, the attempt to list discrete entities in serial fashion, is a typically Western, analytical method of thought and one which is in fundamental conflict with the multivalent, contextual Non-Western modes of thinking. An example of the latter (which will shed light on the type of index used here) is seen in the so-called saddle-roofed granaries of Indonesia. These are not merely *things*; they also express the *idea* of fertility through their shiplike roofs—a reference to the ship of the dead and thus to the ancestors who control fertility. In addition, each granary functions as a *process* continually reassuring the living of ancestor-benevolence while at the same time reminding the deceased of the unfailing devotion lavished on them by the living.

For this reason, the pages cited below are intended merely to suggest important aspects of entities; no attempt at exhaustive indexing has been made.